THE PRINCIPAL'S GUIDE TO THE Educational Rights of Handicapped Students

T. PAGE JOHNSON

National Association of Secondary School Principals
Reston, Virginia

About the Author

T. Page Johnson is director of administrative services for the Fairfax County (Va.) Public Schools and professor of school law at the University of Virginia. In addition to experience as a high school principal, he has been a teacher at both the junior and senior high school levels and has taught educational law and political science on the faculties of the George Washington University, the University of Virginia, and the Virginia Polytechnic Institute and State University.

Johnson is an active speaker and writer in the field of public school law. He has been on the staff of NASSP national institutes on legal issues and has served as a consultant on student law issues to the American Bar Association, the Department of Defense Schools, and principals' organizations in Virginia and other states. He is the author of several NASSP *Legal Memoranda* and articles on school law in both educational and legal journals.

ISBN 0-88210-179-X

National Association of Secondary School Principals
1904 Association Drive
Reston, Virginia 22091
Executive Director: Scott D. Thomson
Director of Publications: Thomas F. Koerner
Assistant Director of Publications: Carol Bruce
Project Editor: Patricia Lucas George
Technical Editor: Eugenia Potter

Table of Contents

Foreword

It has now been a decade since Congress enacted the Education for All Handicapped Children Act of 1975, better known as Public Law 94-142, and two years more since passage of Section 504 of the Rehabilitation Act of 1973.

Together these two pieces of federal legislation form the groundwork of the law affecting the education of the handicapped in the United States. But despite the number of years that have passed since enactment of these laws, a large number of important legal issues concerning the rights of the handicapped in public school and the consequent obligations of the schools and their administrators have continued to arise, with a constant parade of cases marching through the federal district courts to the U.S. Courts of Appeal, and even to the U.S. Supreme Court.

For this reason, the NASSP has resisted until now the impulse that moved some other organizations to try to assemble a definitive statement on the relevant law in this important area of concern.

Instead, the Association has published a number of briefer pieces in the *NASSP Bulletin* and the *Legal Memorandum* to provide some guidance to members while awaiting what seemed to be an appropriate time to put forth a more comprehensive analysis and set of guidelines for action in this important area.[1]

While questions continue to be raised in the courts, and attempts are being made to modify the basic legislation in Congress, it now appears that the basic outlines of the law affecting the rights of the handicapped in public schools have come into focus, and will remain in place. It therefore seems appropriate to publish a guide to this complex and difficult area at this time, especially for principals and other administrators at the local school level.

This monograph attempts to provide this guidance. It sets forth the background of the problems that produced the federal legislation including a review of the cases brought in the early 1970s, outlines the two basic federal laws themselves and the administrative regulations which the executive branch of the government has adopted for enforcement of the laws, and focuses on the specific substantive rights protected by the law and the limits on those rights. The

1. *See*, e.g., "The Supreme Court and the Education of Handicapped Children," *A Legal Memorandum*, September 1982; "The Supreme Court on Special Education: An Update," *A Legal Memorandum*, November 1985; "Expulsion, Suspension, and the Handicapped Student," *NASSP Bulletin*, April 1984; "Educating the Handicapped The Need for Close Cooperation Between Parents, Administrators," *NASSP Bulletin*, November 1983; "Problems To Avoid and Procedures To Follow in Assessing Handicaps," *NASSP Bulletin*, April 1982; "A Legal Brief: Very Special Education, " *NASSP Bulletin*, November 1981.

guide also addresses the procedural protections provided to the handicapped student under the law.

Having dealt with the program for the handicapped and the laws governing its administration from both the principal's desk and the central office, Page Johnson is uniquely qualified to prepare an accurate, complete, and comprehensible guide for principals on this subject. As the nation begins its second decade of administering education programs under the federal law, it also seems that the shape of that law should remain unaltered enough so that this guide should be useful for at least the decade ahead.

Ivan B. Gluckman
NASSP Director of Legal Services and Government Relations

Preface

Today's public school principal wears many hats. He or she is expected to be the school's chief administrator, the instructional leader, the business manager, the head disciplinarian, an educational philosopher, a counselor to the staff, a surrogate parent to the students, a public relations expert, a talented teacher, and a loyal member of the superintendent's management team.

In the words of Gilbert Weldy, today's principal must strive to be "everything to everybody."[1]

In addition, the principal must be constantly aware of the legal component of public education. The past 25 years have seen both a substantial increase in laws affecting the operation of the public schools and important changes in the substantive legal principles that control the decisions of educational administrators. Keeping abreast of these new legal constraints can be a constant challenge for a principal, but it is a challenge that must be met because the legal milieu in which the public schools operate allows no alternative.

Some of the principal's most complex and difficult problems center on the school's legal obligation to provide an appropriate education for the handicapped student. Special education programs are burdened with an array of legal mandates that do not affect general education programs, and two characteristics combine to make mastery of this part of the law of public education a formidable undertaking.

First, most of the legal principles governing the educational rights of the handicapped have been established within the past 10 years. Not only is this body of law new, it changes at a rapid pace.

In a 1981 study, the National Center for State Courts estimated that litigation involving the educational rights of handicapped students comprised 35 to 40 percent of all civil cases involving the rights of students filed since 1976.[2] The number of these cases is not decreasing.

Second, the law governing special education is unusually complex. In addition to understanding two different federal statutes, each with its own set of administrative regulations, the principal must know the appropriate state laws and regulations and be aware of current and sometimes conflicting court decisions.

1. Gilbert R. Weldy, *Principals: What They Do and Who They Are* (Reston, Va.: National Association of Secondary School Principals, 1979), p.1.
2. Thomas Marvell, Armand Galfo, and John Rockwell, *Student Litigation: A Compilation and Analysis of Civil Cases Involving Students 1977-1981* (Williamsburg, Va.: Naional Center for State Courts, 1981), p. 18.

The objective of this book is to provide the principal with an introduction to the legal rights that federal legislators and federal and state judges have conferred on the handicapped student in the public schools, to give the busy principal, who must be "everything to everybody," a guide to the legal rights of the handicapped student that is both brief enough to be useful and comprehensive enough to introduce some of the salient legal issues.

Remember, however, that special education laws change day by day. Keeping up with the changes is a vital part of understanding the educational rights of handicapped students.

All 50 states now receive federal funds for the education of handicapped students in the public schools. For that reason, two federal statutes, the Education of the Handicapped Act, including the amendments added by Public Law 94-142, and the Rehabilitation Act of 1973 establish the legal framework for public school programs for handicapped children in every state.

These two laws are the primary focus of the book. But each state has its own laws and regulations to implement, interpret, and in some cases expand on the federal requirements. These state laws must be studied and consulted along with the information in this guide.

Finally, the book will achieve one of its goals if it convinces the busy principal of the importance of seeking and obtaining the help of qualified legal counsel whenever necessary. There is no substitute for competent legal advice in any dispute about the education of a handicapped student.

T. Page Johnson

CHAPTER 1

The Legal System and the Handicapped Student

The Exclusion of Handicapped Students from the Public Schools

The statutes and judicial decisions that establish the educational rights of handicapped students comprise a voluminous, complex, and difficult-to-understand body of law that seeks to ensure that every handicapped student in the nation will have the opportunity for a free public school education.

Until a few years ago, however, most handicapped students were excluded from the public schools by the same legal system that today advocates their educational rights. Lawmakers and judges supported the public's decision that most handicapped children should not be educated in the public schools and they created the legal doctrine that made exclusion possible.

Prior to the 1970s, most handicapped children had no legally established right to a public education. They were generally denied access to public schools under state laws that excused them from compulsory attendance and removed from public school officials any legal duty to grant them the same access that non-handicapped students enjoyed.

For example, an Alaska law provided for the exclusion of children with "bodily or mental conditions rendering attendance inadvisable."[1] Nevada's law allowed exclusion when the child's "physical or mental condition or attitude is such as to prevent or render inadvisable his attendance at school or his application to study."[2] Virginia's compulsory attendance statute included an exemption for "children physically or mentally incapacitated for school work."[3]

These and similar laws in other states expressed society's belief that the handicapped child could not benefit from education and that his or her presence in the public schools would have an adverse effect on the welfare of the other students.

State courts did not hesitate to support laws permitting exclusion of handicapped students in the few cases in which their parents sought judicial review. In 1893, a school committee in Massachusetts excluded a handicapped child because he was "so weak in mind as not to derive any marked benefit from instruction and further, that he is troublesome to other children . . . . "[4] When the Supreme Judicial Court of Massachusetts was called upon to review the school committee's legal authority to exclude the student, the justices decided:

> Whether certain acts of disorder so seriously interfere with the school that one who persists in them, either voluntarily or by reason of imbecility should not be permitted to continue in school; is a question which the statute makes it [the school committee's] duty to answer: and if they do their duty, a jury composed of men of no special fitness to decide educational questions should not be permitted to say that their answer is wrong.[5]

In a similar case in Wisconsin in 1919, a local school board excluded a 13-year-old physically handicapped boy with normal mental ability because:

> . . .his physical condition and ailment produces a depressing and nauseating effect upon the teachers and school children; . . . he takes up an undue portion of the teachers time and attention, distracts attention of other pupils, and interferes generally with the discipline and progress of the school.[6]

The Wisconsin Supreme Court recognized that the boy had a constitutional right to attend public school. The court held, however, that the school board had the legal authority, and in this case the duty, to exclude the boy. The court said:

> [The school board] was charged with the responsibility of saying whether this boy should be denied a constitutional right because the exercise of the right would be harmful to the school and to the pupils attending. . . .if his presence in school was detrimental to the best interest of the school, then the board could not, with due regard to their official oaths, refrain from excluding him, even though such action be displeasing and painful to them.[7]

This combination of legislative authorization and judicial approval of the denial of a public school education to handicapped children continued, with some exceptions, into the 1960s.[8]

Early in the 1970s, however, the courts, especially the federal courts, initiated a rapid and remarkable change in the legal system's attitude. The resulting judicial overthrow of well-established legal doctrine on the exclusion of handicapped children from the public schools may have had its antecedents in the United States Supreme Court's landmark decision in 1954 in the school desegregation case, *Brown* v. *Board of Education*.[9]

Equal Educational Opportunity: Brown v. Board of Education

The Supreme Court's willingness to use the Fourteenth Amendment as the legal basis for a dramatic expansion of the constitutional rights of individuals after 1945 led to the legal victories that the civil rights movements of the 1950s and 1960s won for blacks, Hispanics, American Indians, and other minorities.

Although handicapped students did not benefit fully from this constitutional revolution until the 1970s, many believe the judicial origins of their right to a public education lie in the Supreme Court's famous 1954 decision in *Brown* v. *Board of Education*.[10]

If *Brown* v. *Board of Education* offered hope for a new attitude toward the rights of handicapped students, the promise appeared in the Supreme Court's discussion of the importance of educating a child. The Court reversed more than 50 years of adherence to the principle that the Equal Protection Clause of the Fourteenth Amendment was not offended when a state elected to provide "separate but equal" facilities based on race.[11] In a unanimous opinion presented by Chief Justice Earl Warren, the Court ruled ". . .that in the field of public education the doctrine of 'separate but equal' has no place. Separate educational facilities are inherently unequal."[12]

The Justices also described a student's right to an education in words that have become the Constitutional basis for many court decisions on equal educational opportunity.

> Today, education is perhaps the most important function of state and local governments. Compulsory school attendance laws and the great expenditures for education both demonstrate our recognition of the importance of education to our democratic society. It is required in the performance of our most basic public responsibilities, even service in the armed forces. It is the very foundation of good citizenship. Today it is a principal instrument in awakening the child to cultural values, in preparing him to adjust normally to his environment. In these days, it is doubtful that any child may reasonably be expected to succeed in life if he is denied the opportunity of an education. *Such an opportunity where the state has undertaken to provide it, is a right which must be made available to all on equal terms.* (emphasis supplied).[13]

The Supreme Court's final sentence suggests a legal basis for what many now call the right to equal educational opportunity, a right that might be claimed by the handicapped student. Only a year after *Brown* v. *Board of Education*, the editor of the bimonthly newspaper of the National Association for Retarded Children called the readers' attention to the Court's language and expressed the belief that it applied to the handicapped student equally with other minorities.[14]

Equal Protection for Handicapped Students: The PARC and Mills Cases

Some observers of our legal system believe a cycle controls the evolution of new law. The cycle begins with judges' decisions that establish new legal rights or principles. Legislators then incorporate the newly-created rights into statutory law, and the cycle is completed when litigation about the meaning of the statutes gives the courts new opportunities to refine the law.[15]

If creation of the handicapped child's right to a public education followed that process, the two judicial decisions that began the cycle are *PARC* v. *Commonwealth of Pennsylvania*,[16] a suit on behalf of retarded students decided by a United States District Court in Pennsylvania in 1971, and *Mills* v. *Board of Education*,[17] a 1972 decision in favor of all students excluded from access to a public education in the District of Columbia.

Indeed, these two decisions may have started the process that led to the adoption by Congress of the Education for All Handicapped Children Act of 1975.[18]

PARC v. *Commonwealth*, a suit begun by the Pennsylvania Association for Retarded Children (PARC), was a class action in the United States District Court for the Eastern District of Pennsylvania on behalf of all mentally retarded persons between the ages of 6 and 21 who were being excluded from access to a public education by the Commonwealth. The suit's goal was to establish the legal right of the retarded to access to a public education.

PARC attacked the Pennsylvania laws that allowed the Commonwealth (a) to refuse to educate any child whom a public school psychologist certified as uneducable and untrainable, (b) to indefinitely postpone admission to public school of any child who had not reached the mental age of five years, and (c) to exempt the handicapped child from the state compulsory attendance laws.

PARC's attorney was Thomas K. Gilhool, a Philadelphia lawyer experienced in public interest litigation. He argued that the Pennsylvania laws violated the equal protection and due process rights of the retarded under the Fourteenth Amendment and Pennsylvania's Constitution and laws that promised a public education to all young people.[19]

The federal court never had a chance to determine the validity of these claims because Pennsylvania's attorney general surrendered, and the court disposed of the case by adopting a consent agreement negotiated by Gilhool and Pennsylvania officials.

The consent agreement was a stunning victory for PARC. It provided, among other things, that because the Commonwealth had by law undertaken to provide a free public education to everyone, Pennsylvania had a legal obligation to place each mentally retarded child in a free, public program of education and training appropriate to the student's capacity.

The agreement required Pennsylvania's attorney general to issue new legal opinions eliminating the use of state laws to exclude retarded children from access to public education.

The consent agreement also required that all retarded children in Pennsylvania be located and provided with educational services, and that the Commonwealth give parents of handicapped children notice and an opportunity for a hearing whenever the student's educational placement was to be changed and to explain procedures in detail, including the parent's right to obtain access to all of the student's educational records.

As attorney Gilhool emphasized later, the parent could effectively use the right to a hearing to review the appropriateness of the educational program.[20]

In the District of Columbia, seven children who had been labeled as being brain-damaged, mentally retarded, emotionally disturbed, or having behavior problems and who had been denied educational services were the plaintiffs in *Mills* v. *Board of Education*.[21] The plaintiffs, residents of public institutions or living with their parents, sued for their own rights and on behalf of all other school-age students who were being excluded from access to a public education in the District of Columbia. The plaintiffs' attorney alleged there were 18,000 handicapped children in the District of Columbia who were not receiving programs of specialized instruction appropriate to their needs.

The District of Columbia School Board admitted it had a legal responsibility to provide these children with a public education and said it was providing special education programs for at least 3,880 school-age children. But, it estimated that 12,340 handicapped children were not being served during the 1971-72 school year. The only defense the school board offered was that it did not have sufficient funds to provide an education to all handicapped children.

The United States District Court issued summary judgment in favor of the children on August 1, 1972. The court held that the District of Columbia was violating the Due Process Clause of the Fifth Amendment to the United States Constitution by denying handicapped children access to a public education while providing it to other children.

The court relied on the Fifth Amendment because the provisions of the Fourteenth Amendment that were cited by the plaintiffs in the *PARC* case do not restrict the federal government, which has exclusive authority over the District of Columbia. The court ruled, however, that the Due Process Clause of the Fifth Amendment imposes on the District of Columbia the same obligation to provide equal educational opportunity that the Equal Protection Clause of the Fourteenth Amendment imposes on the states.[22]

The Court's order also expanded the educational rights won in the *PARC* case by directing that:

> The District of Columbia shall provide to *each child of school age* a free and suitable publicly-supported education regardless of the degree of the child's mental, physical or emotional disability or impairment. (emphasis supplied)[23]

To carry out this mandate, the court ordered school officials to establish a comprehensive program to locate all handicapped children not being served, and directed the school board to provide the right to a constitutionally adequate prior hearing when deciding on the educational placement of a student and ensure periodic review of the student's status and progress.[24]

The decision expanded on the legal principle established in *PARC* v. *Commonwealth* by extending the right to access to a public education to all handicapped children. The decision in the *PARC* case was limited to retarded children.

The legal implications of the *PARC* and *Mills* decisions stimulated judges and lawmakers in other states to increase the handicapped child's access to the public schools. The courts in several states decided that state law guaranteed educational rights for handicapped children.[25] Litigation to establish the handicapped child's legal right to treatment was filed in the federal courts.[26]

State legislatures responded to the increasing litigation by revising special education laws. A survey conducted by federal officials in 1975 revealed that 37 states altered their special education laws between 1970 and 1975.[27] In some states, the changes guaranteed access to a public education for all handicapped children. In New Mexico, the attorney general referred to the *PARC* decision in an opinion holding that New Mexico's laws on the education of the handicapped, previously considered permissive, were mandatory.[28]

Opening the public schools to all handicapped children required greatly expanded special education programs and sharp increases in school budgets. Advocates for the rights of handicapped children and state education officials turned to the Congress of the United States to find some of the money. The United Cerebral Palsy Association noted in its June-July 1972 issue of *Word from Washington*, that because of the *PARC* decision:

> . . . pressure is mounting in Congress for major Federal funding to states for education of the handicapped. Several bills have been introduced. . . . State governments face prospects of litigation and court orders to serve scores of unserved or poorly served handicapped children. In order to meet the requirements of the courts, state budgets for education of the handicapped will have to be significantly supplemented.

Congress responded to the pressure for more federal money to aid states in educating handicapped children by passing new grant programs and federal laws intended to guarantee legal rights for the handicapped. Two of these laws, Section 504 of the Rehabilitation Act of 1973, and Public Law 94-142, the Education for All Handicapped Children Act of 1975, imposed on the public schools of every state comprehensive legal responsibilities for educating handicapped children, and they have been the statutory basis for hundreds of federal and state court decisions.

Endnotes

1. Alaska Statutes, Title 14, Chapter 30 (1971).
2. Nevada Revised Statutes, Section 392.050 (1963).
3. Code of Virginia, Section 22.275.3 (1973).
4. Watson v. City of Cambridge, 32 N.E. 864, 864 (1893).
5. 32 N.E. 864, 865.
6. Beattie v. Board of Education of City of Antigo, 172 N.W. 153, 154 (1919).
7. 172 N.W. 153, 154.
8. *See*, Elgin v. Silver, 182 N.Y.S. 2d 669 (Sup. Ct. 1958).
9. 347 U.S. 483 (1954).
10. 347 U.S. 483 (1954).
11. Plessy v. Ferguson, 163 U.S. 537 (1896).
12. 347 U.S. 483, 494-495.
13. 347 U.S. 493.
14. *Children Limited*, June 1955, p. 9.
15. James M. Kauffman and Daniel P. Hallahan, eds., *Handbook of Special Education* (Englewood Cliffs, N.J.: Prentice-Hall, Inc., 1981), p. 334.
16. 334 F. Supp. 1257 (1971), modified at 343 F. Supp. 279 (1972).
17. 348 F. Supp. 866 (1972).
18. *See*, *The Education for All Handicapped Children Act of 1975*, House of Representatives Report No. 94-332, 94th Congress, 1st Session (1975).
19. PARC v. Pennsylvania, 343 F. Supp. 279 (E.D. Pa. 1972). Gilhool also asserted that the right to an education was a "fundamental right" for the purposes of Fourteenth Amendment analysis, but the court chose not to decide that claim. 343 F. Supp. 283, n. 8.
20. 343 F. Supp. 279, 302-316. Gilhool's comment is in Frederick J. Weintraub, et al., *Public Policy and the Education of Exceptional Children* (Reston, Va.: Council for Exceptional Children, 1976), p. 20.
21. 348 F. Supp 866 (1972).
22. 348 F. Supp. 866, 878-883. *See*, Bolling v. Sharpe, 347 U.S. 497 (1954).
23. 348 F. Supp. 866, 878.
24. 348 F. Supp. 866, 877-883.
25. *See*, e.g., In Interest of G.H., 218 N.W. 2d 441 (N.Dak. 1974); Robinson v. Cahill, 303 A. 2d 273 (N.J. 1973).
26. Wyatt v. Stickney, 344 F. Supp. 387 (M.D. Ala. 1972).
27. Weintraub, et al., p. 84.
28. Leopold Lippman and I. Ignacy Goldberg, *Right to Education: Anatomy of the Pennsylvania Case and Its Implications for Exceptional Children* (New York: Teachers College Press, 1973), Ch. 7.

CHAPTER 2

Congress and the Education of Handicapped Students

The U.S. Constitution does not grant Congress the legal authority to establish or regulate public schools. This power is one of the many governmental responsibilities the states retained when they adopted the Constitution. It is not, therefore, surprising to find that the number of congressional laws affecting the education of handicapped children is small.

But Congress does have the constitutional authority to spend federal money for the general welfare, and it has used that power to enact laws that affect handicapped adults and children.

In the 1970s, Congress responded to the increasing pressure from advocates of equal rights for handicapped children and to a changing legal situation by approving new federal programs. In 1970, Congress passed the Education of the Handicapped Act, which, among other things, authorized grants to help states expand educational programs for handicapped children.

But the decisions in the *PARC* and *Mills* cases greatly increased the pressure on Congress to spend even more federal money on state public school programs for handicapped children. In the wake of these two decisions, and under the pressure of similar litigation pending in many other states, Congress enacted the two federal laws that have established the legal basis for requiring each state to provide every handicapped child with an appropriate education at public expense.

These two laws, Section 504 of the Rehabilitation Act of 1973 (Section 504)[1] and Public Law 94-142, the Education for All Handicapped Children Act of 1975 (EAHCA),[2] are both based on Congress' power to spend federal money for the general welfare and to regulate the way states use the federal funds they receive.[3]

Congress still lacks constitutional power to regulate directly the public school systems of the 50 states, but it has discovered that its power to spend federal dollars can be used to dictate educational policy.

Section 504 of the Rehabilitation Act

Congress enacted the Rehabilitation Act of 1973, Public Law 93-112, as an expansion of its earlier legislation providing rehabilitation programs for disabled veterans and other handicapped citizens. The United States Supreme Court has said the law ". . . establishes a comprehensive federal program aimed at improving the lot of the handicapped. . . ." The Court went on to say that Section 504 was enacted to further the purposes of the Act.[4] Section 504 provides, in part:

> No otherwise qualified handicapped individual in the United States . . . shall, solely by reason of his handicap, be excluded from participation in, or be denied the benefits of, or be subjected to discrimination under any program or activity receiving federal financial assistance. . . .[5]

Section 504 is not a federal grant program; it does not provide any federal money to aid handicapped persons. Instead, it imposes a duty on every recipient of any federal funds not to discriminate against handicapped persons. Thus, it regulates federal programs and a wide variety of state programs that receive federal funds for the benefit of both adults and children, including educational programs in colleges and public schools. A public school district that is receiving any federal funds is affected by the limitations in Section 504.

In addition to affecting the educational programs of the public schools across the United States, Section 504's prohibitions against discrimination on the basis of handicap govern a school district's employment practices, access to school buildings and other facilities, and the design of new construction. The restrictions of Section 504 apply to a school district receiving federal funding whether or not the district decides to take the federal money available under the EAHCA. A school district that does receive federal aid under the EAHCA and complies with all the requirements of that law must also comply with the requirements of Section 504.

The Department of Health, Education, and Welfare (HEW) did not propose administrative regulations to implement Section 504 until 1976, the same year a United States District Court in the District of Columbia found that Congress had intended regulations to be written and ordered HEW to issue them.[6]

HEW did not complete the Section 504 regulations until after the EAHCA had become law. It therefore tried to coordinate those parts of the Section 504 regulations that applied to public school programs for handicapped children with the requirements in the separate set of regulations it was writing to implement the more detailed EAHCA. The final Section 504 regulations were published in the *Federal Register* on May 4, 1977, and became effective on June 3, 1977.[7]

Principals must know what Section 504 prohibits because it protects many of the substantive rights of handicapped students that are not addressed at all by the EAHCA, and students and their parents may sue in the federal courts to enforce these rights. One United States court of appeals compared the two laws by saying:

> The Rehabilitation Act [Section 504] and EAHCA are entirely different statutes. EAHCA imposes an affirmative duty on recipients of federal funds to provide a free, appropriate education for handicapped children. . . . The Rehabilitation Act, on the other hand, is both broader and narrower than EAHCA. It is broader in the sense that it applies to a wide range of federally funded activities, not just an education. It is narrower in that it is not generally speaking, an affirmative-action statute.[8]

The United States Department of Education's Office for Civil Rights (OCR) is the federal agency responsible for the administrative enforcement of Section 504 as it applies to public school programs. Operating from Washington, D.C., and its regional offices in Boston, New York, Philadelphia, Atlanta, Chicago, Dallas, Kansas City, Denver, San Francisco, and Seattle, OCR attempts to ensure compliance with Section 504 by investigating individual complaints, by conducting compliance reviews, and by monitoring public school programs. Each year in the *Federal Register* OCR publishes an annual operating plan that describes the compliance and enforcement activities it plans to conduct during the year.

OCR's primary enforcement effort is the investigation and resolution of individual complaints. Investigation of a complaint begins when OCR receives a written allegation from a person or organization that a school district is violating Section 504. The complaint may, for example, allege that an individual student or a group of students is not being provided the special education and related services that are required by law. That the school district is operating its special education program in full compliance with the EAHCA does not prevent a parent or organization from filing a complaint alleging a Section 504 violation.

OCR usually sends a letter to the superintendent of schools, stating the general allegations of the complaint, explaining the investigative procedures, and identifying the OCR staff member assigned to conduct the investigation. The staff member then contacts the superintendent or his or her representative to request specific information and to arrange an on-site inspection.

The principal who administers the educational program in question is usually involved in the district's response, which may include both submitting written answers to the allegations and arranging for the OCR staff member to interview school staff members and review student records and other documents during the on-site visit. OCR tries to investigate individual complaints promptly because it is under a court order to complete action within a specific time.[9]

The compliance reviews conducted by OCR include a comprehensive examination of all the local school district's educational programs to be certain they comply not only with Section 504, but also with the other federal antidiscrimination laws for which OCR has administrative enforcement responsibility. OCR may, however, limit a compliance review to issues that it selects.

The Section 504 issues that have recently attracted OCR's interest include local school district procedures:

- For locating and identifying handicapped children
- For notifying parents of rights and services available
- For providing related services
- For disciplining handicapped students
- For providing program accessibility to students with orthopedic and sensory impairments
- For making educational placements and changes in placements of handicapped children.

The school districts chosen by OCR for compliance reviews are usually distributed geographically and across the jurisdictional responsibility of OCR.[10]

OCR's monitoring activities focus on determining if local school districts and other recipients of federal funding are carrying out the written plans they have submitted to OCR. Such plans usually explain the actions the school district is taking to comply with one or more of the several laws under OCR's jurisdiction. The school district's plan may have been required by OCR as the result of its investigation of an individual complaint under Section 504, or because of violations discovered during a compliance review.

If a school does not voluntarily comply, OCR can begin formal proceedings to withhold federal funds from the offending school district. Such proceedings are rare and include extensive due process protections for the school district.

OCR's written reports of Section 504 enforcement activities can help principals because they reveal the agency's view of what the law requires. Remember, however, the courts are not required to follow OCR's views in litigation. The reports of OCR's monitoring activities are available in the form of official policy interpretations, the letters of response that OCR writes to school officials who request interpretation of specific provisions of the law or regulations, the letters of findings that follow compliance reviews or the investigation of individual complaints, and the policy memoranda written on specific issues.

Copies of these documents can be obtained directly from OCR, but a more convenient source is a specialized law reporter entitled *Education for the Handicapped Law Report*,[11] that can be found in some law libraries.

Judicial Enforcement of Section 504: The Right To Sue

Congress did not explicitly provide for judicial enforcement of Section 504 through a "private right of action"—that is, the right of a private citizen to bring a law suit asking a court to redress a violation of the law affecting him or her. Nevertheless, the federal courts have been called upon to determine whether this right is implicit in Section 504. Suits by private individuals who suffer from discrimination prohibited by law have been a traditional and effective way to allow judicial enforcement of federal civil rights laws.

Unlike Section 504, many federal anti-discrimination laws provide explicitly for a "private right of action." Advocates for the handicapped have urged the courts to rule that Congress implied this right under Section 504, because the individual law suit permits the courts to remedy some violations more quickly and thoroughly than could ever be accomplished by seeking to cut off federal funds from the offending agency.

Thus, the way in which the federal courts have resolved the question of congressional intent about "private right of action" has, in large measure, determined the amount of judicial enforcement available under Section 504.

The United States Supreme Court has declined to decide formally whether or not there is a "private right of action" under Section 504.[12] But the Justices have implied to the lower federal courts that cases brought by individuals alleging discrimination forbidden by Section 504 should be permitted. In *Campbell v. Kruse*,[13] for example, the Court returned a case about state tuition grants for handicapped children to a lower federal court with instructions to decide it on the basis of Section 504.

The Supreme Court has also held that a person who claims intentional discrimination that violates Section 504 may bring an action to recover back pay.[14] Both actions indicate the Supreme Court believes a "private right of action" exists, at least in some circumstances.

Most of the United States courts of appeals, noting the implications of the Supreme Court's decisions, have held that individuals may sue to enforce their rights under Section 504. For example, the United States Court of Appeals for the Tenth Circuit, in deciding the case of a student who alleged he was denied admission to a university program because he had multiple sclerosis, reviewed the Supreme Court's decisions and other case law and concluded:

> [Section] 504, . . . must also be read to imply a private right of action if individual handicapped persons are to have effective protection against prohibited discriminatory practices. . . . The explicit language evidencing congressional intent that [Section] 504 created a private right of action indicates that such a cause is to be implied under [Section] 504 on the basis of clear congressional intent, ...[15]

Other United States courts of appeals have agreed with the Tenth Circuit's view of the law.[16]

In most states, therefore, a parent may bring an individual law suit against a school district on behalf of a child alleging discrimination on the basis of handicap. The action may usually be started without exhausting any available administrative remedies.[17] The cases that have resulted from the implied "private right of action" have enabled the courts to participate in the enforcement of Section 504.

Handicapped students have used Section 504 in efforts to assert their legal rights to participate in school activities closed to them by decisions of the principal, other administrators, or the rules of state athletic associations.

For example, two different federal courts have held that Section 504 requires that an otherwise qualified high school athlete with only one kidney be permitted to participate in contact sports despite the school officials' fears about a life-threatening injury.[18]

Another federal court, however, upheld a school official's decision to bar from contact sports two athletes who each had only one good eye.[19] A handicapped student successfully challenged the transfer rule of a state high school athletic association under Section 504,[20] but another handicapped student failed to win relief from the 19-year-old rule in the state of New York.[21]

In an unusual case, a parent won a ruling in the United States Court of Appeals for the Fifth Circuit that Section 504 protects children who are not handicapped from erroneous denial of admission to regular classes.[22]

The Supreme Court has now imposed a specific limitation on future judicial enforcement of Section 504 through individual law suits. In *Smith* v. *Robinson*,[23] the Court held that a plaintiff may not use Section 504 to circumvent the extensive administrative procedures required by the EAHCA if the suit concerns the child's right to a free appropriate public education or other substantive rights protected by the EAHCA. In the Court's words:

> . . . there is no doubt that the remedies, rights, and procedures Congress set out in the EHA are the ones it intended to apply to a handicapped child's claim of a free appropriate public education. We are satisfied that Congress did not intend a handicapped child to be able to circumvent the requirements or supplement the remedies of the EHA by resort to the general anti-discrimination provisions of § 504.[24]

The Supreme Court understood that in a number of earlier cases, plaintiffs had alleged violations of Section 504 as a way of gaining court review of a handicapped child's educational program without going through the administrative due process procedures mandated by the EAHCA. The Court's decision that Congress intended the EAHCA, passed after Section 504, to be the exclusive means for determining a handicapped child's right to a free public education limits future individual suits under Section 504 to those rights of the handicapped not covered by the EAHCA.

Smith v. *Robinson* certainly does not eliminate judicial enforcement of Section 504 because, as noted earlier, its prohibitions go beyond the right to access to a public education that is the heart of the EAHCA. The Supreme Court's holding will, unless additional legislative action is taken by Congress,[25] result in a separation between Section 504 and the EAHCA in future cases.

Those asserting substantive rights protected by EAHCA will reach the courts only after the required administrative process has been completed or waived by the courts. Cases going directly to court under Section 504 will be limited to instances of discrimination not actionable under the EAHCA. Enforcement of Section 504 by the courts will continue to merit the principal's attention, and the holdings in future cases may be more easily understood without the complications of EAHCA claims.

Public Law 94-142: The Education for All Handicapped Children Act

Congress enacted the Education for All Handicapped Children Act of 1975 (EAHCA) as a comprehensive revision of Part B of the Education of the Handicapped Act of 1970. The provisions of the EAHCA, known by most principals as Public Law 94-142, are very different from those of Section 504, which prohibits discrimination on the basis of handicap in all programs receiving federal funds, but does not provide any federal money to aid handicapped persons.

By contrast, EAHCA is a federal grant program that allocates substantial sums of federal money to states and local school districts to pay part of the cost of educating handicapped students in elementary and secondary schools. The EAHCA dramatically expanded earlier federal efforts to encourage the states to provide public school programs for all handicapped children and fulfilled the promises Congress made in the Education of the Handicapped Act of 1970.

The EAHCA is an unusually detailed statute that sets forth a specific, complex, and comprehensive design for the education of handicapped children, a design that states must follow to qualify for the federal funds that the law authorizes.[26]

The EAHCA states that its purposes are:

- To ensure that all handicapped children have available a free appropriate public education within definite times
- To protect the rights of these children and their parents
- To assist states and localities in providing for the education of all handicapped children
- To assess and assure the effectiveness of educational programs.

To accomplish these purposes, Congress increased the amounts of money authorized for programs under Part B of the Education of the Handicapped Act and imposed new requirements on the states. The new requirements demanded that: (a) the state have a policy of assuring a free appropriate public education to all handicapped children, including a deadline of September 1, 1978, for children between ages 3 and 18; (b) the state provide expanded due process rights for parents and children, including the right to appeal disagreements to an independent hearing officer and the right to sue; and (c) the state guarantee the development of an individualized education plan to guide each handicapped student's education.[27]

President Gerald Ford had reservations about the effect of the EAHCA when he signed it on December 2, 1975. He believed it unfortunate that the law promised far more than the federal government would be able to deliver and that its good intentions might be thwarted by some of the unwise provisions it contained.

The President asserted that the supporters of the bill knew very well that the law promised more federal money than would realistically be available to the states, and he regretted that the law contained "a vast array of detailed, complex, and costly administrative requirements which would unnecessarily assert Federal control over traditional state and local government functions."[28]

The Administrative Regulations for the EAHCA

The Department of Health, Education, and Welfare used a comprehensive and unusual process to prepare administrative regulations for the enforcement of the EAHCA. The department publicly recognized that because many of the consequences of the law would not be known until the states had some actual experience with implementation, the initial administrative regulations would be "minimum" regulations to be revised frequently and improved as experience dictated.[29] In addition, the actual wording of many of the EAHCA's very specific and detailed sections was incorporated into the regulations.

The department officials said they tried throughout the development of EAHCA regulations to make them consistent in concept and policy with those parts of the Section 504 regulations that govern elementary and secondary programs for handicapped children.

In some instances, the coordination problem was resolved by providing in the 504 regulations that an educational program could be in compliance with Section 504 by being in compliance with the corresponding provisions of the EAHCA regulations. The department's own analysis of the initial EAHCA regulations admitted, however, that a number of potentially confusing differences remained.

For example, one of the central requirements of the EAHCA regulations is that the states provide a handicapped child a free appropriate public education (FAPE). But the definition of a FAPE contained in the EAHCA regulations is different from that in the Section 504 regulations.[30]

The final EAHCA regulations were originally included in part 121 in Title 45 of the *Code of Federal Regulations*. When the Department of Education was created, the regulations were recodified and can now be found in Title 34 of the *Code of Federal Regulations*, part 300.

Administrative Enforcement of EAHCA: The Office of Special Education Programs

Administrative enforcement of the EAHCA is the responsibility of the Office of Special Education Programs in the Department of Education's Office of Special Education and Rehabilitative Services. A different office within the department, the Office for Civil Rights, handles enforcement of Section 504. This division of enforcement responsibility between two separate agencies contributes to the complexity of the law governing the educational rights of handicapped children. It means that principals and other administrators of special education programs must work simultaneously with two federal bureaucracies that do not always agree on what the law requires.

The Office of Special Education Programs' most important enforcement tool is its power to review and approve the annual program plan that each state must submit to qualify for funding. Under the EAHCA regulations, a state's annual program plan must be a comprehensive document that:

- Includes specific assurances of compliance with the provisions of the EAHCA and detailed descriptions of how the assurances will be carried out
- Gives data about the number of handicapped children identified and the personnel being used and needed
- Includes information about the number of local education agencies that will receive funds
- Explains state procedures for evaluation of program effectiveness.[31]

Personnel in the Office of Special Education Programs can dictate educational decisions to state officials during negotiations about the approval of the state's annual program plan.

The Office of Special Education Programs used to announce policy interpretations and explanations of administrative requirements by issuing *Division of Assistance to the States Bulletins* (*DAS Bulletins*). *DAS Bulletins* stated the agency's views on the meaning of specific parts of the law or the regulations, or clarified administrative reporting details.

Each *DAS Bulletin* dealt with a separate subject, was numbered, and was issued as needed. Copies of *DAS Bulletins* were usually sent to state education officials and can be requested by subject from the Office of Special Education Programs. All of the *Bulletins* are included in Volume 2 of the *Education for the Handicapped Law Report*.

In August 1984, the Office of Special Education Programs began issuing *OSEP Memoranda*, publications designed to provide information about the office and the special education programs under its supervision. Each of these memoranda includes a reference number and the name and telephone number of a staff member who can supply additional information about the subject of the memorandum.

The first *OSEP Memorandum*, No. 84-1, issued on August 22, 1984, to state directors of special education, contained a calendar of regulations issued for Public Law 98-199, the Education of the Handicapped Act Amendments of 1983.

The Office of Special Education Programs also issues policy letters responses to requests for interpretations of a specific part of the law or regulations sent in by individuals, groups, principals, and other special education administrators. These interpretations and explanations are applicable only to the specific facts stated in the question. Nevertheless, a review of policy letters can help a principal estimate how the Office of Special Education Programs might interpret the law's requirements and regulations in a specific case. These policy letters are available from the Office of Special Education Programs, but you must know the date and subject of the letter you want. Again, a more convenient way to review policy letters is to consult Volume 2 of the *Education for the Handicapped Law Report*.

The division of responsibility for administrative enforcement of the EAHCA and Section 504 between the Office of Special Education Programs and the

Office for Civil Rights not only complicates life for principals responsible for special education programs, but also presents some problems to the officials of both agencies.

To prevent conflicting enforcement decisions, the Office of Special Education Programs and the Office for Civil Rights entered into a memorandum of understanding on October 15, 1980, to achieve effective, efficient, and consistent application of the two laws. The memorandum of understanding provides for cooperative procedures for the handling of complaints received, for the exchange of information, for joint review of annual program plans submitted by the states, for cooperative planning for compliance reviews, for mutual assistance in the conduct of investigations, and for joint development of policy.[32]

Judicial Enforcement of the EAHCA: The Right To Sue

Congress, in the EAHCA, provided explicitly for parents to file individual law suits, if necessary, to gain a free appropriate public education for a handicapped child. But it also required parents to complete a specific administrative appeal process before seeking judicial intervention. In the words of the Supreme Court, these administrative procedures:

> . . . effect Congress' intent that each child's individual educational needs be worked out through a process that begins on the local level and includes ongoing parental involvement, detailed procedural safeguards, and a right to judicial review.[33]

Section 615 of the EAHCA revised and expanded the procedural protections that the Congress had adopted in the Education Amendments of 1974 by providing that any parent or guardian with a complaint about the identification, evaluation, educational placement, or free appropriate public education of a child would have the right to an impartial due process hearing. If the state permits the hearing to be conducted at the local level, the parent has the additional right to appeal the decision of the local hearing to the state education agency, which must conduct an impartial review and make an independent decision.

The law also provides that at an independent due process hearing, the parent shall have the right to be accompanied and advised by legal counsel and by individuals with special knowledge about handicapped children; the right to present evidence and to confront, cross-examine, and compel the attendance of witnesses; and the right to a written or electronic record of the hearing. The hearing officer must be impartial and cannot be an employee of a local or state educational agency involved in the education or care of the child.

The decision reached at the independent due process hearing is final unless there is a further appeal by any party. After a parent has exhausted the rights to a local due process hearing and to a state review, he or she may bring a civil action in a state court of competent jurisdiction or in a United States district court.[34]

The EAHCA also stipulates that while administrative due process or judicial proceedings are underway, the handicapped child shall remain in the then current placement unless the state or local educational agency and the parents agree otherwise. If the dispute arises while the child is being considered for initial admission to a public school, the child shall, with the parents' permission, be placed in a public school program until the proceedings are completed.[35]

The right of parents to sue if dissatisfied with the results of the administrative hearings has resulted in a flood of law suits. The National Center for State Courts has estimated that 35 to 40 percent of all the civil actions involving students from 1977 through 1981 were concerned with the educational rights of handicapped children.[36]

The holdings of the courts in these cases have defined, explained, and increased the educational rights of handicapped children, and they continue to be an important source of new law. The significance of some of these cases will be examined in the next chapter.

Endnotes

1. Public Law 93-112, 29 U.S.C. §794.
2. 20 U.S.C. §1401 *et seq.*
3. U.S. Const. art. 1, sec. 8, cl. 1. *See*, Oklahoma v. Civil Service Commission, 330 U.S. 127 (1947) (power to attach conditions to grants).
4. Consolidated Rail v. Darrone, 104 S. Ct. 1248, 1250 (1984).
5. 29 U.S.C. §794.
6. Cherry v. Mathews, 419 F. Supp. 922 (D. D.C. 1976).
7. 42 Fed. Reg. 22676. The regulations are codified in 34 C.F.R. Part 104.
8. Monahan v. Nebraska, 687 F.2d 1164, 1170; *accord*, Timms v. Metropolitan, 722 F.2d 1310 (7th Cir. 1983).
9. Adams v. Bell, No. 3095-70 (D. D.C. 1970).
10. Final Annual Plan for FY 1984, 48 Fed. Reg. 57588 (Dec. 30, 1983). In addition to Section 504, OCR has responsibility for Title VI of the Civil Rights Act of 1964, Public Law 88-352, 42 U.S.C. §2000d *et seq.*, and Title IX of the Education Act Amendments of 1972, Public Law 92-318, 20 U.S.C. §1681 *et seq.*
11. Published by CRR Publishing Co., 421 King St., P. O. Box 1905, Alexandria, Va. 22313.
12. Southeastern v. Davis, 442 U.S. 397 (1979); Consolidated Rail v. Darrone, 104 S. Ct. 1248 (1984).
13. 431 F. Supp. 180 (E.D. Va. 1977), *vacated and remanded*, 434 U.S. 808 (1977).
14. Consolidated Rail v. Darrone, 104 S. Ct. 1248 (1984). *See also*, Cannon v. Chicago, 441 U.S. 677 (1979).
15. Pushkin v. Regents, 658 F.2d 1372, 1380 (1981).
16. *See*, Kampmeier v. Nyquist, 553 F.2d 296 (2d Cir. 1977); NAACP v. Medical Center, 599 F.2d 1247 (3d Cir. 1979); Davis v. Southeastern, 574 F.2d 1158 (4th Cir. 1978); Marvin H. v. Austin, 714 F.2d 1348 (5th Cir. 1983); Miener v. Missouri, 673 F.2d 969 (8th Cir. 1982); Kling v. County, 633 F.2d 876 (9th Cir. 1980).
17. Puskin v. Regents, 658 F.2d 1372 (10th Cir. 1981); Kling v. County, 633 F.2d 876 (9th Cir. 1980); Camenisch v. Texas, 616 F.2d 127 (5th Cir. 1980). *See also*, Cannon v. Chicago, 441 U.S. 677 (1979).
18. Grube v. Bethlehem, 550 F. Supp. 418 (E.D. Pa. 1982) (football); Poole v. South Plainfield, 490 F. Supp. 948 (D. N.J. 1980) (wrestling). *See*, Office of Civil Rights Policy Interpretation No. 5, "Participation of Handicapped Students in Contact Sports" (August 14, 1978), 43 Fed. Reg. 36035, 3 EHLR 251:03.
19. Kampmeier v. Nyquist, 553 F.2d 296 (2nd Cir. 1977). *Contra*, Wright v. Columbia, 520 F. Supp. 798 (E.D. Pa. 1981). One student subsequently won the right to play under state law. Kampmeier v. Harris, 411 N.Y.S.2d 744 (App. Div. 1978).
20. Doe v. Marshall, 459 F. Supp. 1190 (S.D. Tex., 1978), *vacated and remanded*, 622 F.2d 118 (5th Cir. 1980), *cert. denied*, 451 U.S. 993 (1981).
21. Cavallaro v. Ambach, 575 F. Supp. 171 (W.D. N.Y. 1983).
22. Carter v. Orleans Parish, 725 F.2d 261 (5th Cir. 1984).
23. 104 S.Ct. 3457 (1984).
24. 104 U.S. 3457, 3473.
25. Legislation to overcome the Supreme Court's decision is pending in Congress. See H.R. 1523 and S. 415, 99th Cong., 1st Sess. and S. 6014, 98th Cong., 2d Sess.
26. 20 U.S.C. §1401 *et seq.*
27. 20 U.S.C. 1402. A useful comparison of the EAHCA requirements with those of the earlier Education of the Handicapped Act is *An Analysis of P.L. 94-142* (Washington, D.C.: The National Association of State Directors of Special Education, n.d.).

28. Statement by the President upon Signing the Education for All Handicapped Children Act, December 2, 1975, 1 EHLR 11:201.
29. *See*, Proposed P.L. 94-192 Regulations, 41 Fed. Reg. 56966 (December 30, 1976).
30. *See*, Appendix A, Final P.L. 94-142 Regulations, 42 Fed. Reg. 42474 (August 23, 1977).
31. 34 C.F.R. §300.110 *et seq*.
32. *Memorandum of Understanding Between the Office for Civil Rights and the Office of Special Education*, October 15, 1980.
33. Smith v. Robinson, 104 S. Ct. 3457, 3469 (1984).
34. 20 U.S.C. §1415. See remarks by Senator Williams, 121 Cong. Rec. S20432 (November 19, 1975).
35. 20 U.S.C. 1415 (e)(3).
36. Thomas Marvell, Armand Galfo, and John Rockwell, *Student Litigation: A Compilation and Analysis of Civil Cases Involving Students 1977-1981* (Williamsburg, Va.: National Center for State Courts, 1981), p. 18.

CHAPTER 3

The Right to a Free Appropriate Public Education

The heart of the Education for All Handicapped Children Act (EAHCA) is the mandate to the public schools to guarantee a free appropriate public education (FAPE) to every handicapped child. All of the other requirements in the law organize and support the child's right to a FAPE and create legal procedures parents may use to enforce that right.

To understand the handicapped child's right to a FAPE, a principal needs to know how Congress defined that term, how the courts have interpreted Congress' words, and how the EAHCA's requirements have been shaped and changed by judicial applications of the law in specific cases.[1]

The Handicapped Student's Right to a Free Appropriate Public Education

The right to a free appropriate public education is the essential educational right that both the EAHCA and Section 504 seek for handicapped children. To qualify for funds under the EAHCA, a state must have in effect a policy that ensures all handicapped children will receive a FAPE.

The administrative regulations for Section 504,[2] require that any recipient of federal funding operating a public elementary or secondary education program must provide a FAPE to each qualified handicapped person regardless of the nature or severity of the person's handicap. All of the other educational rights the two laws grant to handicapped children support and protect the right to a FAPE.

Because the right to a FAPE is the central provision of the EAHCA, it is not surprising that the United States Supreme Court's first decision on the meaning of the EAHCA, *Board of Education of the Hendrick Hudson Central School District* v. *Rowley*[3] required the Court to decide exactly what level of educational services must be provided to a handicapped child to constitute a FAPE. The Supreme Court's decision was significant in the lower courts' later development of the law.

The case began when officials of the Hendrick Hudson Central School District,

Peekskill, N.Y., were requested by the parents of Amy Rowley, a deaf child, to provide a sign language interpreter in Amy's first grade classroom. To help them decide on appropriate services for Amy, school officials heard testimony from Amy's parents, received reports from teachers and others familiar with Amy's academic and social progress, and visited a class for the deaf. The school district's committee on the handicapped finally concluded that Amy did not need the services of an interpreter.

The committee's decision may have been influenced by the experience of a sign language interpreter who had worked with Amy on a trial basis when she was in kindergarten. He reported that Amy had been resistant to his services and did not need them in her kindergarten class. The committee on the handicapped recommended Amy continue using the special FM hearing aid the school district had provided, and that she receive the services of a speech therapist three hours a week. Amy also benefited from her excellent lip reading skills.

Amy's parents initiated due process proceedings and filed suit in the United States District Court when the hearing officer and the New York Commissioner of Education upheld the school district's decision.

The district court found Amy, by that time a second grader, to be a remarkably well-adjusted child who was communicating well with her classmates, achieving an extraordinary rapport with her teachers, performing better than the average child in her class, and advancing easily from grade to grade. Notwithstanding all that success, the court held that she was not receiving a FAPE without the services of the sign language interpreter.

In a remarkable judicial disregard of the facts, the court ruled that the job of defining a FAPE had not been done by Congress but had been left completely to hearing officers and to the federal courts. Acting on that view, the District Court ruled that to guarantee a FAPE, a school district must provide an educational program that permits a handicapped child "an opportunity to achieve his full potential commensurate with the opportunity provided to other children."[4]

Although the court found that Amy was receiving an adequate education without the interpreter, it believed that she could not have an opportunity to achieve her full potential without the aid of the interpreter.[5] A divided United States Court of Appeals sustained this decision,[6] and the school district asked for review by the United States Supreme Court.

The Supreme Court reversed the lower court decision and completely rejected the definition of a FAPE adopted by the District Court. The Justices said:

> . . . Certainly the language of the statute contains no requirement like the one imposed by the lower courts—that states maximize the potential of handicapped children "commensurate with the opportunity provided to other children." . . . That standard was expounded by the District Court without reference to the statutory definition or even to the legislative history of the Act.[7]

The Supreme Court examined the EAHCA and determined that Congress had included a specific definition of a FAPE. The statute provides:

> The term "free appropriate public education" means special education and related services which (A) have been provided at public expense, under public supervision and direction, and without charge, (B) meet the standards of the State education agency, (C) include an appropriate preschool, elementary, or secondary school education in the State involved, and (D) are provided in conformity with the individualized education program required under section 1414(a)(5) of this title.[8]

The statute also defines the meaning of the "special education" and the "related services" that are the components of a FAPE. According to Congress, "The term 'special education' means specially designed instruction . . . to meet the unique needs of a handicapped child."[9] "Related services" are defined as: ". . . transportation, and such developmental, corrective, and other supportive services as may be required to assist a handicapped child to benefit from special education. . . ." Speech pathology and audiology, psychological services, physical and occupational therapy, recreation, and counseling services are specifically included as "related services"; medical services are limited to those necessary for evaluation and diagnostic purposes.[10]

The Supreme Court found the statutory definition of a FAPE to be helpful in interpreting the law, but it also examined the legislative history of the EAHCA to determine if Congress intended to prescribe any additional substantive standard for the education to be provided for a handicapped child. The Court concluded that the intent of the law "was more to open the door of public education to handicapped children on appropriate terms than to guarantee any particular level of education once inside."[11]

The Supreme Court also rejected the Rowleys' argument that the goal of the EAHCA was to provide equal educational opportunity to every handicapped child. That interpretation of the law, said the Court, would establish an "entirely unworkable standard requiring impossible measurements and comparisons."[12]

The Justices explained that if "equal" were understood as requiring the states to provide for handicapped children only those services given to non-handicapped children, the requirements of the EAHCA would not be met. On the other hand, if "equal" were to mean that the handicapped child was to receive every service necessary to maximize his potential, that would go beyond what Congress intended. The Court concluded that the term FAPE was too complex to be captured in the word "equal," whether referring to access or to services.[13]

Although the Supreme Court ruled that Congress did not intend the EAHCA to maximize the handicapped child's potential, as the District Court had ruled, the Justices recognized that Congress intended a FAPE to include *educational services that would benefit the handicapped child*. The Court declined, however, to set any one standard for determining the adequacy of educational benefits under the EAHCA because it recognized that the wide spectrum of handicapped children covered by the law made that task almost impossible for a court to accomplish.

The Supreme Court finally concluded that a state's obligation to provide a FAPE can be described in these words:

> Insofar as a State is required to provide a handicapped child with a "free appropriate public education," we hold that it satisfies this requirement by providing personalized instruction with sufficient support services to permit the child to benefit educationally from that instruction. Such services must be provided at public expense, must meet the State's educational standards, must approximate the grade levels used in the State's regular education, and must comport with the child's IEP.[14]

Employing this definition of a FAPE, the Supreme Court decided the lower courts had erred in ordering the sign language interpreter for Amy Rowley. She was already receiving a program of personalized instruction and related services that was benefiting her educationally. Accordingly, the Justices reversed the decision of the Court of Appeals.

The Supreme Court's decision in *Board of Education* v. *Rowley* has been of seminal importance in shaping lower courts' subsequent interpretations of the EAHCA. As we examine some of the important lower court decisions that have been rendered since *Rowley*, the significance of the Supreme Court's definition of a FAPE and the impact of its comments about the intent of the statute will be apparent.

Placement of Handicapped Students in Private Schools at Public Expense

Can all handicapped children receive a FAPE in the regular public school classroom with special support? Or, must some of them be taught in special schools for handicapped children or in private schools with facilities designed to serve their specific handicaps?

These questions are central to some of the most difficult cases that reach the courts. In some instances, the child's parents are seeking a private school placement despite assurances from public school administrators that the child can receive a FAPE in a public school program designed to accommodate the child's handicap. To resolve these law suits the courts must frequently decide both questions of sophisticated educational methodology and of legal procedure.

Cases that involve children with multiple handicaps so severe they require extensive medical and custodial care in addition to an educational program raise difficult legal issues about the obligation of a school district to provide a FAPE to every handicapped child. The cases of children who require services 24 hours a day raise the question of the school district's legal obligation to pay for residential care when most of the services the child receives are not educational but are essentially life support services.

The case of Daniel Abrahamson illustrates both the legal issues and human compassion concerns that arise in litigation about severely handicapped children.[15]

Daniel was 15 years old, multiply handicapped, and suffering from severe mental retardation, emotional problems, and medical disorders. His seizures required continuous medication, and his kidney condition had to be monitored and treated periodically. School officials offered to provide educational services during the day to Daniel in a 12-month program operated by the public schools, but his parents believed that only a 24-hour residential program could appropriately meet his educational needs. They sued after a due process hearing officer concluded the day program offered by the school was appropriate for Daniel.

The United States District Court found Daniel had a mentality of a one to four-year-old child, and that he could not speak, dress, eat, go to the bathroom, or otherwise care for himself unaided. The judge described his coping mechanisms as "autistic like."[16]

Expert testimony from several psychologists said that Daniel needed 24-hour reinforcement of the behavior modification techniques being used in his educational program in order to make progress. Evidence also established that his program should include special attention to correcting his running away behavior and his inability to recognize dangerous situations.

Based on the evidence it heard, the court ruled that the school district must provide either a 24-hour residential placement or a suitable residential arrangement for Daniel, such as a community group home, with specialized staff to support and reinforce the daytime educational program. The judge was convinced that the residential component of Daniel's life was vital to any educational progress and therefore the school district must provide it one way or another.

School officials appealed to the United States Court of Appeals for the First Circuit, arguing that the school district should not be held responsible for providing the residential portion of Daniel's needs when almost all of the services he would receive would be custodial care not related to his educational deficits.

The court of appeals said that in accordance with *Rowley*, the school district cannot be required to provide residential services for a handicapped child simply to enhance an otherwise sufficient day program of education. The court argued that residential placement is not required when the child can make educational progress in a day program; residential placements cannot be ordered to remedy a poor home situation or to make up for some other deficit not covered by the EAHCA because Congress did not intend to burden school districts with providing all the social services to every handicapped child.

In Daniel Abrahamson's case, however, the court of appeals believed the question was whether or not he could make any educational progress at all in the absence of a program of around-the-clock training and reinforcement. The court concluded that the evidence proved that Daniel would not make any progress unless placed in a program with the residential support and 24-hour reinforcement he needed. The court said:

> To be sure, what Daniel will be taught in a residential program . . . will concern skills of daily life, subjects that are not normally covered in ordinary curriculums. But, it is hard to disagree with the Third Circuit's statement that "the concept of education is necessarily broad with respect to" some profoundly retarded children. . . . Where what is being taught is how to pay attention, talk, respond to words of warning, and dress and feed oneself, it is reasonable to find that a suitably staffed and structured residential environment providing continual training and reinforcement in those skills serves an educational service for someone like Daniel.[17]

The First Circuit thus adopted the rule that when a child's educational needs, defining that term quite broadly, require a residential placement for him or her to make any progress, the school district must provide that placement. A number of other federal courts have reached similar conclusions.[18]

School districts are not required, however, to place handicapped children in private schools or residential facilities at public expense if they can provide the student an appropriate educational program in the public schools. Recognizing this general rule, the United States Court of Appeals for the Fourth Circuit held that public school administrators are not under a legal obligation to consider in every instance the availability and appropriateness of nonpublic educational services before recommending a public school program for a handicapped child.[19] Instead, the court said that private placements should only be considered when no appropriate public school program is available.

> While the federal and state statutory schemes clearly contemplate the use of nonpublic educational services under some circumstances, we think it clear that such resort is limited to those instances in which public educational services appropriate for the handicapped child are not available.[20]

Education in the Least Restrictive Environment

Under what circumstances does the EAHCA permit a school district to educate a handicapped child in special classes, schools, or facilities that serve only handicapped children? When the courts speak of the EAHCA's strong preference for "mainstreaming," do they mean the same thing that principals and special educators mean when they talk about mainstreaming?

Judicial decisions provide some of the answers to the first question. The answer to the second question is no; educators usually attach a different and more limited meaning to the term "mainstreaming" than do the courts.

Principals and special education personnel may use the word "mainstreaming" to describe the part of a handicapped child's educational program carried out in a regular general education class with nonhandicapped students. In this sense, a handicapped student who spends half of his or her school day in a regular general education fourth grade class for nonhandicapped students and the other half of the day in a special class for handicapped students may be described as being 50 percent mainstreamed. When the courts use the word "mainstreaming," they almost always refer to a specific section of the EAHCA, which they say expresses "a strong preference" for mainstreaming.[21].

The section in the EAHCA to which the courts refer says:

> . . . to the maximum extent appropriate, handicapped children, including children in public or private institutions or other care facilities, are educated with children who are not handicapped, and that special classes, separate schooling, or other removal of handicapped children from the regular educational environment occurs only when the nature or severity of the handicap is such that education in regular classes with the use of supplementary aids and services cannot be achieved satisfactorily.[22]

Notice that the language does not impose an absolute requirement that handicapped children be taught in the regular classroom in every case. Instead, it requires that arrangement "to the maximum extent appropriate." This explains the courts' statement that the law expresses a strong preference for mainstreaming.

The statutory language is supported by more detailed provisions in the regulations. The regulations use the term "least restrictive environment" to explain that schools must offer a continuum of alternative placements and must educate the student in the school he or she would attend if not handicapped unless his or her IEP requires another arrangement.[23]

The decision of the United States Court of Appeals for the Ninth Circuit in the case of *Department of Education of Hawaii* v. *Katherine D.*[24] illustrates how the courts enforce the law's preference for mainstreaming.

Katherine was an elementary school-age child who suffered from cystic fibrosis and tracheomalacia, a condition requiring her to use a tracheostomy tube to breathe and to expel mucus secretions from her lungs two or three times a day. Although she was unable to speak normally, she had received speech therapy and was learning to talk very softly.

Hawaii officials offered a program of homebound instruction for the school year 1980-81, including speech therapy and parent counseling. They believed, based on the opinion of their physician, that Katherine's medical problems could not be accommodated in the regular public school program. Her parents refused this offer and continued to send her to the private school she had been attending before becoming eligible for special education services from the public schools and where her mother was a teacher. They also began due process procedures to obtain reimbursement for the cost of tuition at the private school. When a hearing officer ruled in favor of the parents, the state sought judicial review.

While her appeal was underway, the state proposed a new IEP for Katherine for the school year 1981-82. It recommended placement of Katherine in a local public elementary school where the teaching staff would meet her daily medical needs. School administrators proposed training teachers to care for Katherine's tracheostomy tube and to dispense the medication she needed.

The United States District Court for Hawaii concluded that the program of home instruction offered for 1980-81 did not comply with the EAHCA because it failed to provide education in the least restrictive environment.[25] The state appealed.

The Ninth Circuit Court of Appeals agreed that the homebound instruction program offered for 1980-81 was not a FAPE because it did not propose to educate Katherine with nonhandicapped children. The court said Katherine's attendance in a regular class at a private school for more than a year demonstrated that she was capable of participating in regular classes with nonhandicapped children. The homebound program offered by the public school was therefore inappropriate.

The court of appeals also held that Katherine's medical needs associated with her tracheostomy tube fell within the range of the related services that the school must provide.[26]

The EAHCA's preference for mainstreaming can also become a legal issue when parents want a handicapped child placed in the regular classroom with support services even though the school administrators believe the child cannot be taught there and must be placed in a special class for handicapped children. The United States Court of Appeals for the Sixth Circuit has adopted guidelines for enforcing the mainstreaming requirement that strongly favor placement of even severely handicapped children in the regular classroom.[27]

Neill Roncker, a nine-year-old severely retarded child, also suffered from seizures that had to be controlled by medication. Evidence showed that Neill operated at a mental age of two or three for most purposes. Although he was not a danger to other students, he did require almost constant supervision because of this inability to recognize when he was in danger.

School personnel wanted to place Neill in a special school for the retarded where he could receive appropriate supervision, but where he would have no daily contact with nonhandicapped children. Neill's parents wanted him in a class for the severely mentally retarded in a regular public school where he would be with nonhandicapped children during lunch, physical education, and recess. School officials pointed out that Neill had been placed in the kind of educational program advocated by his parents but failed to make any progress. The dispute eventually reached a United States district court.[28]

District Judge Carl Rubin eloquently described the problem that almost every judge faces when called upon to decide a case involving the appropriate educational placement for a handicapped child:

> The issue presented here, however, appears to be less in the discipline of law and more in the fields of neurology, child psychology and education. The Court had the benefit of expert opinions. They were in all instances detailed and comprehensive. They were also essentially contradictory. There are, it appears, differing schools of thought sincerely subscribed to by outstanding individuals regarding the treatment of a retarded child.

> A court of law is equipped only to determine legal rights established by statutes, precedents and rules of evidence. Within these limitations, a fair and just society may be fashioned. A perfect society, however, will not.[29]

Notwithstanding this frustration, Judge Rubin concluded that Neill Roncker's case had to be decided on the legal meaning of the phrase "to the maximum extent appropriate" in the law's mainstreaming requirement. He held the phrase does not impose a mandatory duty to educate all handicapped children in an integrated environment with nonhandicapped children.

In Neill's case, the court said the preponderance of the evidence proved he could not be appropriately educated in a class for the mentally retarded in the regular school even with supplemental aids. Judge Rubin was clearly influenced by Neill's failure to make any educational progress when previously placed in a special class in a regular school. He decided the case in favor of the school officials by declining to set aside the proposed placement in the school for the retarded.

Neill's parents appealed to the United States Court of Apeals for the Sixth Circuit. It reversed Judge Rubin's decision and sent the case back to the lower court to be reconsidered using specific guidelines to determine when placement in a segregated facility is permissible.

The court of appeals said the EAHCA's language directing that handicapped students be educated with nonhandicapped students to the "maximum extent appropriate" expressed a very strong congressional preference for mainstreaming. The preference for mainstreaming extends, according to the court, to nonacademic activities such as lunch, gym, recess, and transportation to and from school.

The appellate court said that when a school district proposes to place a child in a segregated facility serving only handicapped students, the judge must determine whether or not the educational arrangements that make the more restrictive placement appropriate for the child's educational needs can possibly be provided in another setting that would allow contact with nonhandicapped children. If they can, a placement in the segregated facility would violate the mainstreaming preference of the law. The court of appeals wrote:

> In a case where the segregated facility is considered superior, the court should determine whether the services which make the placement superior could feasibly be provided in a non-segregated setting. If they can, the placement in the segregated school would be inappropriate under the Act. Framing the issue in this manner accords the proper respect for the strong preference in favor of mainstreaming while still realizing the possibility that some handicapped children simply must be educated in segregated facilities either because the handicap would not benefit from mainstreaming, because any marginal benefits received from mainstreaming are far outweighed by the benefits gained from services which could not feasibly be provided in the non-segregated setting, or because the handicapped child is a disruptive force in the non-segregated setting.[30]

The Sixth Circuit also ruled that lower courts may consider cost when applying its mainstreaming guidelines, because excessive spending on one handicapped child will deprive other handicapped children. The lower courts should not, however, allow cost to be a defense when the school system failed to use its funds to provide a continuum of alternative placements for handicapped children.[31]

The appeals court ordered the lower court to consider whether Neill's educational, physical, or emotional needs required some service which could not feasibly be provided in a class for handicapped children in a regular school or in a combination program that would allow him some daily contact with non-handicapped children.[32]

Other federal courts have adopted a more balanced approach when considering school personnel recommendations that a handicapped child's special needs justify removal from the regular classroom. The Court of Appeals for the Ninth Circuit sustained the decision of an Arizona school district to send a physically handicapped girl, suffering from cerebral palsy but of normal intelligence, to school in another district where she could be taught by a special education teacher certified in physical disabilities.[33] School personnel emphasized that the school the girl would be attending was only 30 minutes away and that she had not been making any progress in the local school.

The girl's parents alleged a violation of the mainstreaming requirements of the EAHCA, but the Ninth Circuit said that although the law did have a preference for mainstreaming, it must always be balanced with the need to provide the child with an appropriate education. In this case, the court of appeals held that the objective of mainstreaming would not be violated by giving the child special instruction from a teacher particularly suited to deal with her learning problems.[34]

Perhaps the most unusual judicial interpretation of what is required by the mainstreaming provisions of the EAHCA came from a United States district court in Texas.[35]

The case concerned the need for a student to be taught in an air-conditioned environment. Raul Espino, paralyzed in the lower part of his body, was confined to a wheelchair as a result of injuries received in an automobile accident before he was a year old. His sympathetic nervous system was also damaged in a way that prevented his body from conserving or dissipating heat normally. Because of his condition, Raul could not be exposed to excessive heat without becoming physically ill; he spent almost all of his early childhood indoors in an air-conditioned environment with little or no opportunity to interact with other children.

Raul attended kindergarten in an air-conditioned classroom at a special school for the handicapped, where he experienced no medical problems attributable to his unusual condition. When it came time for him to move to first grade, school personnel decided the special school was too restrictive for his educational needs; they recommended placement in a regular first grade class with non-handicapped children. Because the regular elementary schools had no air-conditioned classrooms, school officials attempted to arrange a place for Raul in one of the local private elementary schools that had air-conditioned classrooms, but none of the schools would accept him as a student.

The superintendent of schools finally decided to arrange for a portable, air-conditioned Plexiglas cubicle to be constructed for Raul's use within a non-air-conditioned first grade classroom. The superintendent later justified his decision to build the cubicle by explaining that: (a) the school district could not afford to air-condition the whole classroom; (b) he anticipated many problems with other students, parents, and teachers if only the classroom used by Raul were air-conditioned; and (c) Raul did not need air-conditioning all the time to control his body temperature, so the cubicle would permit him to use the air-conditioned environment only when necessary.

Raul's parents pressed for air-conditioning the whole classroom, but the administrative hearings they requested supported the superintendent's decision. While the administrative due process was underway, Raul completed his first grade year using the cubicle. He spent up to 75 percent of his classroom time inside the cubicle during the hot months in the fall, was able to be outside the cubicle for most of the time during the winter and early spring, but had to return to the cubicle beginning in mid-April. At first, his cubicle had no sound system, and Raul could not hear the teacher while inside; later, a one-way radio receiver was installed to permit him to listen to instructional activities.

The case eventually reached a United States district court. Judge F. B. Vela began his analysis by holding that air-conditioning was clearly a related service required to permit Raul to attend school during the hot months. He said the law's mandate that Raul be educated "to the maximum extent appropriate" with nonhandicapped children required the court to determine if the air-conditioned classroom the boy needed could be provided.

Finding no evidence that the school district could not afford the cost of air-conditioning the whole classroom (estimated to be $5,700), and no testimony that a fully air-conditioned classroom would be harmful to either Raul or his classmates, Judge Vela concluded that the use of the cubicle was a violation of the EAHCA's preference for mainstreaming.[36]

The Right to Related Services

The EAHCA says a FAPE includes both special education and related services. School administrators and parents have frequently disagreed about the scope of the requirement to provide related services, and the courts have been asked to resolve these disagreements. The legal issues have been important enough to attract the attention of the United States Supreme Court.

The EAHCA defines related services as:

> . . . transportation, and such developmental, corrective and other supportive services (including speech pathology and audiology, psychological services, physical and occupational therapy, recreation, and medical and counseling services, except that such medical services shall be for diagnostic and evaluation purposes only) as may be required to assist a handicapped child to benefit from special education, and includes the early identification and assessment of handicapping conditions.[37]

The administrative regulations for the EAHCA contain detailed definitions of some of these terms (speech pathology, audiology, etc.), require that the student's IEP list the related services he or she is to receive, and extend the definition of related services to include ". . . school health services, social work services in schools, and parent counseling and training."[38] The federal officials who interpret the regulations have said the related services a school district must provide are not limited to those specifically mentioned in the statute and regulations, but must be determined individually for each child.[39]

The United States Supreme Court has established three guidelines for deciding when a handicapped child is entitled to related services.

- The child must have a handicap that requires special education services.
- A school district is required to provide only those related services necessary to aid the child in benefiting from special education.
- School nursing services must be provided only if they can be performed by

a nurse or other qualified person; any services that must be performed by a physician are not included.[40]

A school district is obligated to provide only those related services that a handicapped child needs to benefit from the special education he or she is receiving. Determination of the related services an individual child needs is a part of the IEP process. Nevertheless, related services is a fertile area for disagreements between school administrators and parents because the cost of furnishing some related services is very high and the variety of services that some parents have requested at public expense under the rubric of related services is amazing.[41]

In relatively few cases have the courts been asked to resolve disputes over transportation, recreation, occupational therapy, and physical therapy as related services.[42]

The more perplexing and legally complex issues have reached the appellate courts when parents have demanded that the school district pay for or actually provide medical treatment or life support services for a handicapped student. These cases have presented the courts with hard questions. Are such services "supportive services" within the meaning of the law? If so, what are the limits, if any, on the kinds of medical or life support services that school districts must provide to a handicapped student to allow him or her to benefit from special education?

School administrators have sometimes refused to pay for or provide medical and life support services for a handicapped student, asserting that they are not legally required to do so and that already hard-pressed educational budgets cannot support the high cost of medical services for the student. They have pointed to the EAHCA statement that medical services are considered related services only when they are for diagnostic or evaluation purposes.

The Pennsylvania Secretary of Education, for example, expressed his fear that if the courts expand the definition of related services to include what he called "ameliorative health services," schools would be faced with a duty to provide such things as transfusions, medication administration, orthopedic devices, iron lungs, and renal dialysis machines.[43]

By declining to provide medical or life support services with public school funds, school administrators do not deny the student's needs. They stress that because these services are medical and not educational in nature, the cost should be borne by the student's parents or through the aid of public social service agencies if necessary. Educational dollars, they believe, must be spent for educational programs.

Specific cases may also reflect the reluctance of teachers and other professional staff to be responsible for actually giving medical or life support services to a handicapped student. Teachers point to the risk to the student's welfare when educational staff who have no medical qualifications are asked to perform medical procedures, and they worry about the potential legal liability if the student is injured in some way.

These valid concerns, balanced against the student's needs, present the courts with sensitive philosophical and legal issues in litigation about related services.

The case that reached the United States Supreme Court, *Irving Independent School District* v. *Tatro*,[44] began in Irving, Texas, in 1979. Amber Tatro, a three-year-old child, suffered from myelomeningocele, usually called spina bifida, and from a neurogenic bladder, a condition requiring clean intermittent catheterization (CIC) about every three or four hours.

Amber was, of course, too young to perform this procedure for herself, and her parents sued when the school district refused to provide it for her as a related service while she was attending the early childhood development program for handicapped children.

The United States District Court recognized that Amber's plight tugged at the heartstrings, but also realized its interpretation of the related services requirement in the EAHCA might have far-reaching consequences for other school districts in hundreds of different situations.

Congress did not, according to the court, intend the language of the law to be so broad where related services were concerned. To qualify as a related service, the court said, the need for the service must arise from the effort to educate. Related services include only those services that enhance the handicapped child's ability to learn, and the term was not intended to require that school districts provide life support services such as CIC.

To support its interpretation, the court pointed out that Congress included in the definition of related services a specific limitation saying that medical services are related services only when required for diagnostic and evaluation purposes. The court rejected the plaintiff's claim that CIC was a related service by finding instead that it was a life support service for Amber and was not "related" to her special education in the sense Congress intended.

The judge apparently feared that a decision in favor of Amber would require school districts to supply every life support service any handicapped child might need while at school. The court ruled that neither the EAHCA nor Section 504 required the school district to provide CIC for Amber.[45]

On appeal, the United States Court of Appeals for the Fifth Circuit reached a very different conclusion about the nature of related services.[46] The court held CIC to be a related service for Amber because without it she would be unable to attend school and therefore unable to benefit from the special education to which she was entitled.

The court of appeals also found the school system's refusal to provide CIC to be a violation of Section 504. The lower court's fear that school districts might be called upon to supply an unlimited array of medical and life support services to handicapped children was unfounded, in the opinion of the court of appeals, because the law does limit the life support services that can be required.

The Fifth Circuit vacated the lower court decision,[47] and, when further proceedings in the case resulted in the school district being ordered to provide CIC for Amber,[48] school officials convinced the United States Supreme Court to review the case.[49]

The Supreme Court said that to decide if CIC is a related service under EAHCA, two questions must be answered: Is CIC a "supportive service" required to assist a handicapped child to benefit from special education? Should CIC be excluded from the related services requirement because it is a medical service for other than diagnostic and evaluation purposes?

The Court concluded that the answer to the first question must be yes. CIC is a "supportive service" when, as in Amber's case, it is necessary to permit the child to attend school and thereby benefit from special education. It said: "A service that enables a handicapped child to remain at school during the day is an important means of providing the child with the meaningful access to education that Congress envisioned."[50]

The Supreme Court also agreed with the court of appeals that CIC is not a medical service that should be excluded from the category of related services. The Court pointed out that the EAHCA regulations defined "medical services" as those "provided by a licensed physician,"[51] and also stated that related services must include "school health services provided by a qualified school nurse or other qualified person."[52]

The Court found that school nurses had long been a part of the services provided to all students and therefore the regulations were reasonable in requiring school districts to provide school health services to handicapped children as a related services. According to the Court, "It would be strange indeed if Congress, in attempting to extend special services to handicapped children, were unwilling to guarantee them services of a kind that are routinely provided to the nonhandicapped."[53]

The Court found that in Amber's case, CIC could be performed by a school nurse or even by a trained lay person; it was not necessary to have a licensed physician do it. CIC was, therefore, a valid related service for her.[54]

The Supreme Court emphasized the limits to its decision and attempted to allay fears that school districts might be required to pay for a vast array of medical services to handicapped children under the related services mandate.

First, the Court said that only students sufficiently handicapped as to require special education could claim related services, and then only if the services were required to permit the child to benefit from the special education. Thus, if a handicapped student needs medication or treatment that could be given outside school hours, the school district is under no obligation to provide school health services to administer it.

Second, the Court said any service that must be performed by a licensed physician is excluded from the related services the school district may be asked to provide.

Finally, the Court implied that the school has no obligation to provide any specialized equipment that the child may require in connection with the related services being requested.[55]

The Supreme Court's decision in *Tatro* settles the issue of CIC as a related service. More important, the Court's opinion includes some helpful guidance for determining whether other requests are within the medical services exclusion or must be allowed as a part of the school health services to which handicapped students are entitled.

Must school districts provide psychotherapy as a related service? The question presents a variation on the issues the courts faced in deciding about CIC and other life support services. Psychotherapy may be a medical service and, as we have seen, the statutory definition of related services limits medical services to those required for diagnostic and evaluation purposes. On the other hand, the law's definition specifically includes "psychological services, . . . and counseling services," terms that some argue encompass psychotherapy.[56]

The EAHCA clearly designates educational counseling and psychological services such as test administration and interpretation related services that must be provided if the handicapped student needs them. Educational counseling and psychological services, however, are not usually given by persons with medical qualifications. Psychotherapy, on the other hand, is customarily provided by or under the supervision of a medical doctor. Is it, therefore, medical treatment that is excluded from the definition of related services?

The issue is further confused by the apparent lack of any standard, generally-accepted definition of psychotherapy in either the mental health or legal professions.[57]

Federal officials responsible for interpreting the EAHCA and Section 504 regulations have been unable to agree about whether psychotherapy is or is not a related service. The Bureau of Education for the Handicapped (BEH), the federal office in the Department of Education responsible for interpreting the EAHCA regulations before the creation of the Office of Special Education Programs (SEP), contended that if state law interpreted psychotherapy as a medical service—that is, one administered by a licensed physician—the school district would not be required to provide it.

If, on the other hand, the state defines psychotherapy as a "counseling service," school officials would be required to provide it as a related service for a handicapped child.[58] BEH apparently had second thoughts about this position because it later told another school district the question was "under study."[59]

The Office for Civil Rights, responsible for enforcement of Section 504, has consistently said psychotherapy is required as a related service because it is a "psychological service."[60]

Only a few courts have addressed the issue, but the judges' decisions reflect the disagreements of the administrative officials and use similar reasoning. Consider, for example, the opinion of a United States district court in New Jersey in the case of an emotionally disturbed student who had been placed, by agreement between the parents and the school district, in the Child Day Hospital, a specialized treatment program for seriously emotionally impaired children.[61]

All students in the program were required to participate in "therapeutic treatment" for a portion of the day. Hospital officials considered the treatment, which included individual psychotherapy as well as family and milieu therapy on an integrated basis, to be a critial part of their program; no child could be in the program without participating in the therapeutic treatment. The federal courts became involved when the school district refused to pay the costs of the therapeutic treatment part of the child's program, amounting to more than $25,000 during a two-year period.

School administrators based their refusal to pay for the therapeutic treatment on the stated policy of the New Jersey Department of Education that psychotherapy is not a related service under the EAHCA, and that it was not included in the IEP that the school board and the parents agreed on. But the child's parents responded that psychotherapy is a related service and in this instance was an integral part of the educational program in which the school district agreed to place the child.

To reach its decision, the court reviewed the findings of two other courts[62] that, prior to the Supreme Court's decision in *Rowley*, concluded that psychotherapy is a related service.

Then, with an eye on the language in *Rowley*, the court said in this case psychotherapy was both a required part of the program and an essential service to allow the child to benefit from the educational program. It was not, in the court's view, part of a package intended to maximize his performance and therefore was not barred by *Rowley*.

To the argument that psychotherapy cannot be required because it is a medical service, the court said:

> In fact it is undisputed here that the so-called psychotherapy which D. G. received at the Hospital, while administered under the supervision of a trained psychiatrist, was actually provided on a day-to-day basis by a staff member with no more credentials than a Masters in Social Work degree. Thus D. G.'s therapy might be described equally appropriately as "counseling services" or "psychological counseling"—both of which are specifically included by the regulations among the "related services" required. . . .[63]

Exactly the opposite conclusion was reached by another United States district court in Illinois, where local school administrators and the parents had agreed to place a child with a severe behavior disorder in a psychiatric hospital in another state.[64] The state board of education, however, refused to approve the placement. The state contended that psychiatric treatment received in the hospital was medical treatment and therefore not a related service under the EAHCA. The child's parents sued, asserting that the state's refusal to approve the placement denied the child a FAPE in violation of both EAHCA and Section 504.

Federal District Judge John A. Nordberg ruled that the refusal to pay for placement in the psychiatric hospital did not violate either the EAHCA or Section 504. He relied on the Supreme Court's language in *Rowley*, saying a state is not required to provide a child with the best possible educational placement. He emphasized that Illinois' refusal of this particular placement did not deprive the child of access to a FAPE, and that school officials had provided an appropriate alternative placement during pending litigation.

Rowley, according to the judge, does not permit lower courts to order school officials to pay for any services not explicitly required by the statute. The court rejected the argument that psychotherapy can come within the "psychological services" mentioned in the EAHCA's definition of related services: "Psychiatrists in contradistinction to psychologists, counselors and other providers of psychological services, are licensed physicians whose services are appropriately designated as medical treatment."[65] Judge Nordberg also denied the Section 504 claim by ruling that Section 504 does not impose any greater requirements than the EAHCA.

A United States district court in the District of Columbia adopted a similar view of psychotherapy when it held that a school district was not required to fund the placement of an emotionally handicapped child in a private psychiatric hospital. The court found the placement was for medical treatment and not to support a special education program for the child.[66]

Where do these conflicting interpretations of the law by both the regulatory agencies and the courts leave the principal who faces parents' requests that psychotherapy be provided as a related service?

Regrettably, there are no easy answers. Each child's case must be considered individually and with careful attention given to both the state education policy and to the provisions of state law controlling how psychotherapy may be provided. Principals should seek the advice of legal counsel before establishing policy on psychotherapy and when making decisions about individual cases.

Graduation Competency Tests

Many states require all students to pass a minimum competency examination to qualify for high school graduation. The programs have provoked litigation on behalf of both nonhandicapped and handicapped students.[67]

The federal courts have generally affirmed the power of a state to impose minimum competency requirements, but they also have insisted on certain basic protections for all students.[68]

When state minimum competency requirements are applied to handicapped students, judges may face this question: does requiring a handicapped student to pass the minimum competency examination to receive a diploma deny that child a FAPE? Both federal and state courts have answered that question and have decided other legal challenges to graduation testing requirements for handicapped children.

An influential case arose in Peoria, Ill., when the school district mandated that every student pass a minimum competency test to qualify for a standard high school diploma.[69] The case illustrates both the impact of the *Rowley* decision on this issue and how litigation over the educational rights of handicapped children can include claims under the Fourteenth Amendment as well as EAHCA and Section 504.

Peoria required every student to achieve a minimum score of 70 percent on each section of the three-part examination in reading, language arts, and mathematics to earn a standard high school diploma. The examination was given each semester; a student who failed any part was permitted to repeat the test until he or she passed it or reached 21 years of age. Refresher courses were available at no cost during the school year and for a tuition charge in the summer.

A student who had all the requirements for graduation but had not passed the examination might elect to receive a Certificate of Program Completion at graduation and continue to take the examination until age 21. The testing program was adopted by the school board in February 1978, became effective with the class of 1980, and applied to both nonhandicapped and handicapped students seeking a standard high school diploma.

A group of handicapped students challenged the requirement, and the case eventually reached the United States Court of Appeals for the Seventh Circuit. The students alleged: (a) that the minimum competency examination violated their rights under the EAHCA by denying them a FAPE, (b) that it violated Section 504 because it constituted discrimination based on a handicap, and (c) that it abridged their rights under the Due Process Clause of the Fourteenth Amendment because it was implemented without adequate advance warning.

To decide the students' claim under the EAHCA, the court of appeals looked to the Supreme Court's definition of a FAPE in *Rowley*, especially its statement that the "intent of the Act was more to open the door of public education to handicapped children on appropriate terms than to guarantee any particular level of education once inside."[70]

The court of appeals concluded that this meant the EAHCA did not guarantee any specific results from the education provided to a handicapped child. For that reason, the court of appeals held that handicapped children who had been receiving special education and related services as required by the EAHCA, but who did not achieve an education level that would enable them to pass the minimum competency examination and therefore were denied a diploma, were not denied a FAPE.[71]

The court of appeals also rejected the students' claim that requiring the examination was a discrimination based on their handicaps and in violation of Section 504. The court was guided by an earlier Supreme Court decision holding that: (a) an "otherwise qualified" person under Section 504 is one who is able to meet all the requirements of a program in spite of a handicap and (b) an educational institution is not required by Section 504 to make substantial modifications in a program to accommodate a handicapped person.[72]

The court of appeals concluded that Peoria was not obliged by Section 504 to alter the content of the examination to accommodate a handicapped student's ability or inability to learn the material. The court held that neither the contents of the examination nor the requirement that handicapped children pass it to qualify for a standard high school diploma violated Section 504.

But the court cautioned that the examination must not be administered to handicapped children in a way that would prevent them from showing their knowledge. A blind child, for example, would have to be given the examination in Braille or orally to comply with Section 504.[73]

The students' argument that the examination requirement violated the Due Process Clause of the Fourteenth Amendment because it was begun without adequate advance notice to them presented the court of appeals with a more complex legal question.

The court noted that judges in two other cases had reached different conclusions about the amount of advance warning the Due Process Clause demands when students will be required to pass an examination to qualify for a diploma.[74]

In this instance, the students received notice of the requirement more than a year before it became effective. Nevertheless, the court of appeals ruled that the students did not get adequate advance warning and were thus deprived of their due process rights protected by the Fourteenth Amendment.

The court based its holding, in part, on the failure of the educational programs prescribed by the students' IEPs to prepare them for the examination. Earlier notice of the testing requirement would have permitted the students and their parents to decide whether or not the students' IEPs should have been modified to include goals and objectives for passing the examination and would have allowed enough time to achieve those goals.[75]

In summary, the Seventh Circuit Court of Appeals upheld Peoria's decision to require handicapped students to pass the same minimum competency examination required of other students so long as the handicapped student is given adequate notice of the requirement and the examination is administered with modifications appropriate to the student's handicap.

The state courts in New York have also sustained the application to handicapped students of a statewide program of minimum competency testing, and the United States Supreme Court has declined to review the decision.[76]

Education for More Than 180 Days a Year

Does a handicapped child have a right to a year-round education at public expense even though the state limits nonhandicapped children to 180 days of schooling a year? Does a state policy limiting all children to a maximum of 180 days of instruction a year violate the requirement that a handicapped child must be provided a FAPE?

Litigation about these questions has arisen in Pennsylvania, Georgia, Missouri, and Mississippi, and has resulted in decisions by several United States courts of appeals.

The first and most publicized case challenging a state limit on the number of days a year a student can receive free public schooling started as a class action in a United States district court in Pennsylvania.[77] The suit attacked the refusal of Pennsylvania officials to fund an educational program for any handicapped child for more than 180 days a year.

The plaintiffs in the case included handicapped children who were severely and profoundly impaired, severely emotionally disturbed, orthopedically handicapped, and severely mentally retarded; some of them were attending 12-month residential programs and others were day students in both public and private schools.

The plaintiffs alleged Pennsylvania's policy of limiting all students in the Commonwealth to a maximum of 180 days a year of free public schooling constituted a denial of a FAPE under the EAHCA and violated their legal rights under Section 504 and the Due Process and Equal Protection Clauses of the Fourteenth Amendment.

The district court based its decision on the EAHCA and did not reach the plaintiffs' other legal claims. The court examined the legislative history of the EAHCA and decided that Congress intended the law to ensure educational services to handicapped children that would leave them, on completion of school, as free as possible from dependency on others, within the limits of their handicapping condition. To achieve that goal, the law required that special education be designed to meet the handicapped student's unique needs.

The court concluded that Pennsylvania's policy of limiting educational services for handicapped children to 180 days a year, regardless of their needs, was a denial of a FAPE because the unique needs of some handicapped children, including the plaintiffs, required longer educational programs.[78]

Pennsylvania appealed to the United States Court of Appeals for the Third Circuit, which also held that the state's policy was a violation of the EAHCA because it might deny a handicapped child a FAPE. The court of appeals said:

> We believe the inflexibility of the defendants' policy of refusing to provide more than 180 days of education to be incompatible with the Act's emphasis on the individual. Rather than ascertaining the reasonable educational goals, and establishing a reasonable program to attain those goals, the 180-day rule imposes with rigid certainty a program restriction which may be wholly inappropriate to the child's educational objectives. This, the Act will not permit.[79]

The United States Supreme Court declined to review this case,[80] thus leaving the court of appeals decision standing as the law in the Third Circuit. The court's opinion has also influenced decisions of three other federal appellate courts in similar cases. The judges in these later cases also had the benefit of the Supreme Court guidance in the *Rowley* case, which had not yet been decided when the Third Circuit ruled against Pennsylvania's 180-day policy.

Georgia's policy of applying a 180-day rule to educational programs for handicapped children was challenged by the Georgia Association of Retarded Citizens (GARC) in a class action on behalf of all mentally retarded school age children who needed more than 180 days of instruction to meet their unique needs.

The plaintiffs alleged the state's policy violated the EAHCA, Section 504, the Equal Protection and Due Process Clauses of the Fourteenth Amendment, and Georgia law.

The case, *Georgia Association* v. *McDaniel*,[81] was before the United States Court of Appeals for the Eleventh Circuit when the Supreme Court decided *Rowley*. The court of appeals, therefore, had to consider if the definition of a FAPE provided in *Rowley* required a decision different from that of the Third Circuit in the Pennsylvania case.

The Eleventh Circuit noted that in *Rowley* the Supreme Court said the intent of the EAHCA was "more to open the door of public education to handicapped children on appropriate terms than to guarantee any particular level of education once inside."[82] Nevertheless, the court followed the reasoning of the Third Circuit in the Pennsylvania case. It held that limiting educational programs for retarded children to 180 days violated the demands of the EAHCA that a handicapped student's individual needs be considered.

The Eleventh Circuit rejected the state's argument that Congress' failure to mention any duration of services in the law should be interpreted as an intent to require only the traditional nine-month school year. The court of appeals ruled the state's policy also violated Section 504.[83]

The United States Court of Appeals for the Eighth Circuit has also considered the effects of *Rowley* on state policies limiting programs for handicapped students to 180 days a year. In *Yaris* v. *Special School District*,[84] the court of appeals sustained the decision of a United States district judge to enjoin Missouri's refusal to consider more than 180 days of instruction for severely handicapped children because the refusal denied the children a FAPE.[85] Evidence in the case revealed that summer programs were provided to certain other handicapped children and to some nonhandicapped children.

The Eighth Circuit also agreed that the district judge was correct when he refused to order an extended school year for any of the plaintiffs but instead ordered state officials to consider each child's needs for more than 180 days of instruction. The court of appeals said that *Rowley* requires "access to specialized instruction and related services which are individually designed to provide educational benefits to the handicapped child."[86]

A United States district court in Mississippi took a different view of Congress' intent in the EAHCA when it upheld the state's refusal to provide more than 180 days of special education. This court believed the law only covered the kind and quality of services a state must provide to a handicapped child; it ruled that questions of duration of services were left completely to the states to decide.

The United States Court of Appeals for the Fifth Circuit reversed the decision of the District Court.[87] The court of appeals said the Supreme Court's decision in *Rowley* made clear that an appropriate education included "the requirement that the education to which access is provided be sufficient to confer some educational benefit upon the handicapped child."[88]

The court said Mississippi's categorical refusal to consider special education programs beyond 180 days prevented a determination of which students required year-round programs in order to receive the educational benefit the law promised them.

These decisions by four different United States courts of appeals illustrate that state policies limiting the educational programs of all handicapped children to 180 days a year will not withstand judicial scrutiny. These cases do not, however, require that all handicapped children be provided year-round educational programs. The decision about which students need the additional schooling must be made individually in keeping with the emphasis in the EAHCA on an individual determination of a handicapped student's needs.

Endnotes

1. To avoid confusion in this discussion, the initials of the Education for All Handicapped Children Act of 1975, EAHCA, refer to all the requirements in the federal Education of the Handicapped Act of 1970 (EHA), as amended. Some courts do likewise, but others use the initials EHA when speaking of these same legal requirements. The latter is technically correct because the EAHCA took the form of an amendment to the already existing EHA. Supra, Ch. 2.
2. 34 C.F.R. §104.33.
3. 483 F. Supp. 528, 483 F. Supp. 536 (S.D. N.Y. 1980), *aff'd.*, 632 F.2d 945 (2nd Cir. 1981), *rev'd*, 102 U.S. 3034 (1982).
4. Rowley v. Board of Education, 483 F. Supp. 528, 534.
5. 483 F. Supp. 528 (S.D. N.Y. 1980).
6. 632 F. Supp. 945 (2nd Cir. 1981).
7. 102 S.Ct. 3034, 3042.
8. 20 U.S.C. §1401(18).
9. 20 U.S.C. §1401(16).
10. 20 U.S.C. §1401(17).
11. 102 S.Ct. 3034, 3043.
12. 102 S.Ct. 3034, 3047.
13. *Ibid.*
14. 102 S.Ct. 3034, 3049.
15. Abrahamson v. Hershman, No. 80-2513-K (D. Mass. January 22, 1982), *aff'd.*, 701 F.2d 223 (1st Cir. 1983).
16. 1981-1982 EHLR DEC. 553:516.
17. 701 F.2d 223, 228 (1st Cir. 1983). The Third Circuit decision referred to is Kruelle v. New Castle, 642 F.2d 687 (3rd Cir. 1981).
18. *E.g.*, Kruelle v. New Castle, 624 F.2d 687 (3rd Cir. 1981); North v. District of Columbia, 471 F. Supp. 136 (D. D.C. 1979); Stacey G. v. Pasadena, 547 F. Supp. 61 (S.D. Tex. 1982).
19. Hessler v. Maryland, 700 F.2d 134 (4th Cir. 1983).
20. 700 F.2d 134, 138.
21. Department of Education v. Katherine D., 727 F.2d 809, 817 (9th Cir. 1984). *See also*, Roncker v. Walter, 700 F.2d 1058, 1063 (6th Cir. 1983), *cert. denied*, 104 S.Ct. 196 (1983); and Board of Education v. Rowley, 102 S.Ct. 3034, 3049 (1982).
22. 20 U.S.C. §1412(5).
23. 34 C.F.R. §§300.550-300.554.
24. 727 F.2d 809 (9th Cir. 1984).
25. 531 F. Supp. 517 (D. Hawaii 1982).
26. 727 F.2d 809, 815.
27. Roncker v. Walter, 700 F.2d 1058 (6th Cir. 1983), *cert. denied*, 104 S.Ct. 196 (1983).
28. Roncker v. Walter, No. C-1-80-90 (S.D. Ohio, July 21, 1981), 1981-82 EHLR DEC. 553:121.
29. 1981-82 EHLR DEC. 553:123.
30. 700 F.2d 1058, 1063.
31. *See also*, Age v. Bullit, 673 F.2d 141 (6th Cir. 1982).
32. 700 F.2d 1058, 1063.
33. Wilson v. Marana Unified School District, 735 F.2d 1178 (9th Cir. 1984).
34. *See also*, Johnston v. Ann Arbor, 569 F. Supp. 1502 (E.D. Mich. 1983); Troutman v. School District of Greenville County, C.A. No. 82-2759-14 (D. S.C. March 11, 1983).
35. Espino v. Besteiro, 520 F. Supp. 905 (S.C. Tex. 1981).
36. *Ibid.* The decision was appealed by the parents on the issue of attorney's fees. Espino v. Besteiro, 708 F.2d 1002 (5th Cir. 1983).
37. 20 U.S.C. §1401(a)(17).
38. 34 C.F.R. §§300.13 and 300.346. Related services may be classified as special education if state law defines them as special education. 34 C.F.R. §300.14(a)(2).
39. Policy letter to Irving Levine, August 23, 1979, 2 EHLR 211:122.
40. Irving Independent School District v. Tatro, 104 S.Ct. 3371, 3379 (1984).

41. Sharon Howard, "What Constitutes a Related Service?" *Schools and the Law of the Handicapped* (rev. ed., National School Boards Association, 1981), p. 69.
42. *See, e.g.*, Maurits v. Board, Civ. B-83-1746 (D. Md. 1983) (physical therapy); Rettig v. Kent, 539 F. Supp. 768 (N.D. Ohio, 1981), *aff'd in part, vacated and remanded in part*, 720 F.2d 463 (6th Cir. 1983) (occupational therapy and extracurricular activities); Birmingham and Lamphere School Districts v. Superintendent, 328 N.W. 2d 59 (Mich. App. 1982)(recreation); Hurry v. Jones, 560 F. 500 (D. R.I. 1983), *aff'd in part, reversed in part*, 734 F.2d 879 (1st Cir. 1984) (transportation).
43. Petitioner's Brief for Certiorari, Scanlon v. Tokarcik, 102 S.Ct. 3508 (1982), 1981-82 EHLR DEC. 553:307.
44. 481 F.Supp. 1224 (N.D. Tex. 1979), *vacated and remanded*, 625 F.2d 557 (5th Cir. 1980), *on remand*, 516 F. Supp. 968 (N.D. Tex. 1981), *aff'd.*, 703 F.2d 823 (5th Cir. 1983), *aff'd in part and reversed in part*, 104 S.Ct. 3371 (1984).
45. Tatro v. Texas, 481 F. Supp. 1224 (N.D. Tex. 1979).
46. Tatro v. Texas, 625 F.2d 557 (5th Cir. 1980).
47. 625 F.2d 557 (5th Cir. 1980). *See also*, Tokarcik v. Forrest Hills, 665 F.2d 443 (3d Cir. 1981), *cert. denied sub. nom* Scanlon v. Tokarcik, 102 S.Ct. 3508 (1982).
48. Tatro v. Texas, 516 F. Supp. 968 (N.D. Tex. 1981), *aff'd*, 703 F.2d 823 (5th Cir. 1983).
49. 104 S.Ct. 523 (1983).
50. 104 S.Ct. 3371, 3377.
51. 34 C.F.R. 300.13(b)(4).
52. 34 C.F.R. 300.13(b)(10).
53. 104 S.Ct. 3371, 3378.
54. 104 S.Ct. 3371, 3377-3378. The Court, based on its decision in Smith v. Robinson, 104 S.Ct. 3457 (1984), reversed the Fifth Circuit's holding that Amber was also entitled to relief, including an award of attorney's fees, under Section 504. The Court declined to decide whether CIC might also be within the "supplementary aids and services" that school districts must provide to allow handicapped children to be taught in regular classrooms. *See*, 20 U.S.C. §1412(5)(B).
55. 104 S.Ct. 3371, 3379.
56. 20 U.S.C. 1401(17).
57. *See*, "Psychotherapy as a 'Related Service'," *Education for the Handicapped Law Report*, Supplement 60 (November 13, 1981), p. AC15. 1981-82 EHLR DEC. AC15.
58. Policy letter to Raphael Minsky, April 7, 1978, 2 EHLR 211:19.
59. Policy letter to Robert F. Millman, June 5, 1979, 2 EHLR 211:104; policy letter to T. D. Beck, November 6, 1979, 2 EHLR 211:145.
60. Complaint letter of findings to Berkley Unified School District, July 26, 1979, 3 EHLR 257:191; complaint letter of findings to Connecticut Department of Education, October 17, 1979, 3 EHLR 257:57.
61. T. G. v. Board of Education, 576 F. Supp. 420 (D. N.J. 1983), *petition for cert. filed*, September 19, 1984 (No. 84-461.)
62. Papocoda v. Connecticut, 528 F. Supp. 68 (D. Conn. 1981); In the Matter of the "A" Family, 602 P.2d 157 (Mont. 1979).
63. 576 F. Supp. 420, 424.
64. Darlene L. v. Illinois, 568 F. Supp. 1340 (N.D. Ill. 1983).
65. 568 F. Supp. 1340, 1344.
66. McKenzie v. Jefferson, 566 F. Supp. 404 (1983).
67. *See*, Debra P. v. Turlington, 730 F.2d 1405 (11th Cir. 1984) (due process and equal protection challenge by nonhandicapped students).
68. Debra P. v. Turlington, 474 F. Supp. 224 (M.D. Fla. 1979), *aff'd in part, vacated and remanded in part*, 644 F.2d 397 (5th Cir. 1981). *See*, Martha M. McCarthy, "Minimum Competency Testing on Trial," 13 *Education Law Reporter* 191.
69. Brookhart v. Illinois, 534 F. Supp. 725 (C.D. Ill. 1982), *rev'd* 697 F.2d 179 (7th Cir. 1983).
70. 102 S.Ct. 3034, 3043.
71. 697 F.2d 179, 183.
72. Southeastern Community College v. Davis, 442 U.S. 397 (1979).
73. 697 F.2d 179, 183-184.
74. Debra P. v. Turlington, 474 F. Supp. 224 (M.D. Fla. 1979) (holding one year inadequate notice), *aff'd in part, vacated and remanded in part*, 644 F.2d 397 (5th Cir. 1981); Board of Education v. Ambach, 458 N.Y.S. 2d 680 (App. Div. 1982) (holding three years adequate notice).
75. Brookhart v. Illinois State Board of Education, 697 F.2d 179 (7th Cir. 1983). *See*, Anderson v. Banks, 540 F. Supp. 761 (S.D. Ga. 1982) (24 months held to be adequate notice).

76. Board of Education v. Ambach, 469 N.Y.S. 2d 669 (Ct. App. 1983), *cert. denied*, 104 S.Ct. 1598 (1984).
77. Armstrong v. Kline, 476 F. Supp. 583 (E.D. Pa. 1979).
78. 476 F. Supp. 583, 604-605.
79. Battle v. Commonwealth, 629 F.2d 269, 280 (3rd Cir. 1980).
80. Scanlon v. Battle, 452 U.S. 968 (1981).
81. 716 F.2d 1565 (11th Cir. 1983).
82. 102 S.Ct. 3034, 3042.
83. Georgia Association v. McDaniel, 716 F.2d 1565 (11th Cir. 1983), *vacated and remanded*, 104 S.Ct. 3581 (1984).
84. 728 F.2d 1055 (8th Cir. 1984).
85. Yaris v. Special School District, 558 F. Supp. 545 (E.D. Mo. 1983).
86. 728 F.2d 1055, 1056.
87. Crawford v. Pittman, 708 F.2d 1028 (5th Cir. 1983).
88. 102 S.Ct. 3034, 3048.

CHAPTER 4

The Right to Due Process

Congress included comprehensive procedural safeguards in the Education for All Handicapped Children Act (EAHCA) to ensure that state and local school districts make appropriate decisions when identifying and placing handicapped children and to allow parents a process for appeal if they disagree with the decisions.

Many of the specific requirements had already been adopted by Congress as part of the Education Amendments of 1974.[1] In the EAHCA, these procedural safeguards were strengthened and expanded to provide comprehensive protection for the rights of the handicapped child.

The EAHCA requires state and local school districts to adopt procedures that guarantee:

- The parent's right to inspect all the educational records of the child,[2]
- The right to obtain an independent educational evaluation of the child,[3]
- The appointment of surrogate parents if necessary,[4]
- The parental right to prior notice of their rights,[5]
- The right to file complaints and have them resolved by an impartial due process hearing,[6]
- The right to a state review of the hearing held at the local level.[7]

As the last procedural safeguard, Congress provided that either the parent or the school district may seek judicial review of the final administrative decision.[8]

This chapter examines these procedural safeguards and the courts' interpretation of them.[9]

The Right To Examine Records

The EAHCA section that requires the school district to provide the handicapped child's parents with an opportunity to inspect all of the child's relevant educational records supplements other provisions of the law and regulations that provide parents with extensive privacy rights in connection with school records.[10]

The EAHCA requires the Secretary of Education to act in accordance with the provisions of the Family Educational Rights and Privacy Act of 1974 (FERPA)[11] to assure the confidentiality of personally identifiable information in educational records. The EAHCA regulations on confidentiality go beyond the requirements that the FERPA makes applicable to all students.

The EAHCA regulations, for example:

- Apply to some children not covered by the FERPA
- Provide parents with more extensive access rights
- Cover any agency engaged in the identification, location, evaluation, or education of handicapped children
- Expand parental consent requirements for the release of records
- Provide more details on the storage and safeguarding of records
- Establish specific procedures for the destruction of records when they are no longer needed.

Other requirements under the EAHCA not found in the FERPA are the stipulation that one official must assume responsibility for the confidentiality of personally identifiable information, that all persons collecting and using personally identifiable information receive training on confidentiality procedures, that the school district maintain for public inspection a list of all persons with access to personally identifiable information, and that rules governing the destruction of records must be followed.

A Delaware court has ruled that a handicapped child's surrogate parents have access to school records[12] and a federal court in New York has affirmed that educational records must be released in response to a lawful subpoena.[13]

But the most significant court decision may have come from a United States district court when the parents of a student no longer receiving special education services requested destruction of all records relating to the child's previous enrollment in special education classes for the learning disabled.

The court ruled the section of the EAHCA regulations governing destruction of records at parental request did not deny school officials the discretionary power to decide that the records should not be destroyed because they might be educationally useful in the future.[14]

The Right to Prior Notice

The EAHCA requires a written prior notice to the parents before a school district proposes to initiate or change, or refuses to initiate or change, the identification, evaluation, or educational placement of the student or the provision of a free appropriate public education (FAPE) to the child. The law also requires that the notice inform the parents fully, in the parents' native language, of the procedural safeguards available under the law.

The written prior notice must also include:

- A description of the action that the school district proposes or refuses to take

- An explanation of the reasons for the decision
- A description of the options the school district considered and the reasons they were rejected
- A description of each test or report used as a basis for the decision
- Any other information relevant to the school district's proposal or refusal.[15]

Federal officials issued a policy letter to explain these requirements.[16] Among other things, the letter attempts to clarify the confusion surrounding exactly what tests must be described in the prior notice sent to parents.

The prior notice for a preplacement evaluation does not have to include a list of the tests that will be used. The requirement to describe an evaluation procedure or test applies to those already given and those that are the basis for the school district's decision. The notice for a preplacement evaluation does, however, have to describe the records, reports, or tests that caused the school district to propose the evaluation.

After the evaluation is conducted, and school officials propose to make an initial placement in a special education program, the prior notice for that proposed placement must include a description of the tests given that led officials to propose that placement.

The prior notice requirements can cause principals some perplexing problems in determining exactly what must be included in the written prior notice and when it must be given to the parent. The requirements in the EAHCA and regulations make clear that the contents of the prior notice must fit the specific decision or recommendation the school district is making. The notice must also be individualized to the parent receiving it because the regulations require it be provided in the parents' native language.

If the parent speaks a language without a written form, school officials must maintain written records that prove the notice was given orally and that the parent understood. Clearly, the prior notice contemplated by the EAHCA may have to be given to the parent several different times in slightly different forms. A single, written prior notice form given to all parents may not meet the legal requirement.

The importance of giving the parent a legally correct prior notice is illustrated by a case decided in a United States district court in North Carolina.[17]

James Hall, IV, a student of apparently above average intellectual ability, experienced difficulties with reading from the time he entered elementary school. He repeated the second grade, but he was still reading at a second grade level when he reached the fifth grade.

At the beginning of his third grade year, school officials conducted extensive psychological testing with the permission of James' parents but without sending Mr. and Mrs. Hall the full written prior notice of their rights as required by the EAHCA.

Two years later, James was evaluated again and a new IEP was proposed, again without the required notice of rights to his parents. James reached the fifth grade without any improvement in his reading, and his learning problems were causing him to develop a school phobia. His parents finally had him privately tested and discovered that his problem was dyslexia, a condition the school district's testing had failed to uncover.

The Halls placed James in a private school specializing in teaching children with his disability and later brought suit against the school district to recover the expense of the private testing and the cost of James' tuition at the private school.

In analyzing the case, the federal judge acknowledged that courts do not usually allow parents to recover the cost of a private school placement for a handicapped child when the parents make the placement unilaterally and without the consent of the school district.[18] The court said, however, that the rule against allowing parents to recover reimbursement is predicated on the assumption that the parents have been fully advised of their procedural rights.

In this case, the judge found that the school staff had repeatedly violated the requirement to notify the Halls of all their rights under the law. Had they been notified of their rights at the proper time, they would have been aware of their right to an independent evaluation of James, of their right to appeal through the due process structure, and of the legal duty to maintain James in his current educational placement while any due process was pending.

Because of the school district's failure to give the Halls proper notice of their rights, the court ruled that an exception to the rule against allowing recovery for the cost of unilateral private placements was justified. The judge awarded the Halls more than $30,000 as reimbursement for the costs of the private evaluations for James and his tuition at the private school. He said:

> The disregard of the procedural guarantees which are the foundation of the EHA compels an award of reimbursement for the parents. This is not an isolated failure to meet the procedural requirements of the Act, rather the LEA [local education agency] repeatedly ignored the requirements which help ensure an appropriate education. Had the Halls been informed of all their rights under Section 1415, they also would have been informed of the right to a consensual private placement prior to review and the consequences of unilateral action if consent to a prior placement is not forthcoming. However, where, as here, an egregious violation of the procedural requirements occurs, reimbursement is not barred.[19]

The Right To File Complaints and Have an Independent Due Process Hearing

The key procedural protections afforded parents under the EAHCA are the right to present complaints about their child's educational program and the right to have those complaints decided by an independent due process hearing. These are the rights that Thomas K. Gilhool, attorney for the plaintiffs in the *PARC* case, emphasized are central to enforcing the handicapped student's right to an education that meets his or her individual needs.[20]

The EAHCA requires that the state or the local school district, if designated to do so by state law or by the state education agency, provide an impartial due process hearing. If the state elects to have the due process hearing held by the local school district, it must allow an appeal by either party to the state education agency, which must conduct a review and make an independent decision.

The law thus permits the state to have a two-level system with the impartial due process hearing provided by the local school district but subject to appeal to the state for a review, or a single-level system with the hearing being handled directly by the state. The choice can be made by state law or by the state education agency.[21]

The local hearing officer, and the state reviewing officer when the two-level system is used, may not be an employee of the public agency responsible for providing the hearing. During the hearing, the parents have the right to be represented by counsel and by individuals with special training in the needs of handicapped children; the right to present evidence and to confront, cross-examine, and compel attendance of witnesses; the right to written findings of fact and decisions; and the right to receive an electronic or written record of the hearing.[22]

The regulations extend to school districts the right to request an independent due process hearing, require the school district to inform parents of free or low cost legal and other relevant services available in the area if the parent requests such information or the school district initiates the hearing, and establish other procedures to be followed during the hearing.[23]

The federal courts have been asked to settle a variety of controversies about the right to an independent due process hearing. One question is whether the right to a due process hearing extends to students not currently enrolled in the school district.

The United States Court of Appeals for the Fifth Circuit has upheld the decision of a lower federal court that the right to a due process hearing does extend to a handicapped student who has been withdrawn from the school district's rolls.

The case concerned a 17-year-old educable mentally retarded boy who requested a due process hearing after he had voluntarily withdrawn from school. The court of appeals ruled that the superintendent was wrong to deny the request because the section of the EAHCA that grants the right to a due process hearing to parents of handicapped children makes no exception for students not currently enrolled.[24]

An issue that has attracted the attention of both federal regulatory officials and the courts is the question of who may serve as an independent hearing officer or a state reviewing officer. What exactly did Congress mean when it wrote into the law a prohibition against hearings being conducted by employees of an agency involved in the education or care of the child?

The purpose of the prohibition is, of course, to assure that the person who acts as the hearing officer is totally impartial, but a number of questions have arisen about how the law should be applied in specific cases.

Two federal appellate courts have decided that employees of a state's department of education are not eligible to be hearing officers. The Eighth Circuit Court of Appeals ruled that the state superintendent in Iowa could not serve as a hearing officer for a complaint filed against a local school district.

The superintendent argued that because he was not employed by the local school district he should be eligible to serve. The court held, however, that as state superintendent he was, in the words of the law, "involved" in the education of the child even though his involvement was indirect.[25]

The United States Court of Appeals for the Third Circuit has upheld a lower court ruling that the use of an employee of the state department of public instruction of Delaware as a state-level reviewing officer violated the statute.[26]

May a state board of education as a whole, or may one of its members act as a hearing officer? This question arises because members of state boards of education may not be considered employees of the state's department of education under state law. The court decisions are mixed.

A United States district court in Vermont has ruled that a member of the state board of education may be designated as a state review officer because in Vermont the members of the state board are appointed by the governor for fixed terms and are therefore not employees of the state education agency.[27]

On the other hand, the United States Court of Appeals for the Fifth Circuit has concluded that the state board of education in Georgia could not, consistent with the law, conduct the state review of a local hearing decision.[28]

At one time, federal regulatory officials interpreted the EAHCA to allow state education agency employees, chief state school officers, and members of state boards of education to serve as state reviewing officers under certain circumstances. The decisions of the federal courts have caused them to reevaluate their interpretation, but they have not been able to decide on a new position.

The Office of Special Education Programs (SEP) first took the position that employees of the state education agency, chief state school officers, and members of state boards of education were categorically prohibited from serving as local hearing officers or state review officers under any circumstances.[29]

A year later, however, this view was modified to include a presumption that these persons are involved in the education of all the handicapped children in the state and they should therefore not serve as state review officers unless the state has adopted a specific set of procedures to ensure their impartiality.

States were warned that failure to comply with this interpretation might mean disapproval of future state plans and loss of federal funding.[30]

The Due Process Hearing

Any issue relating to the identification, evaluation, or educational placement of the student or the provision of a free appropriate education can be the subject of a due process hearing. The hearing must be provided at the expense of the school district, if the state permits the hearing to be at the local level, and must be scheduled at a time and place mutually convenient to the parties.

The hearing must be held promptly after the receipt of a complaint because the regulations provide that a final decision must be reached by the hearing officer within 45 days from receipt of the request for a hearing unless a specific extension of time is granted at the request of either party. The school district is responsible for ensuring that the deadline is met.

Both parties are entitled to be represented by legal counsel or others with specialized knowledge. The regulations also encourage full disclosure by both parties of all evidence to be presented at the hearing; they provide that either party can prohibit the use at the hearing of any evidence not disclosed to the other party at least five days prior to the hearing.

The parent has the right to have the child present and to open the hearing to the public. At the conclusion of the hearing the parent has a right to receive the written findings of fact and decisions.[31]

When the decision of local hearing officers is appealed by either party to a state review, the state reviewing officer must examine the record of the local hearing, see that the procedures followed were consistent with due process, and make an independent decision in the case within 30 days. He or she may, in his or her discretion, allow the parties to present additional oral or written argument or additional evidence. If the state reviewing officer holds an additional hearing to receive evidence, both parties have all the rights accorded them at a local hearing.

The decision of the state reviewing officer must be final unless either party appeals for judicial review.[32]

Some of the procedures required in due process hearings have been reviewed by the courts. The right of the parent and the school district to be represented by persons with special knowledge who are not attorneys has stirred up some controversy. This provision in the law can run directly counter to some state laws that limit this kind of representation to licensed attorneys.

Federal officials have forced at least one state superintendent of public instruction to back away from a contention that only attorneys may represent the parties at a due process hearing. They argued such a limit is inconsistent with the intent of the federal legislation.[33]

In at least one state, legislation has been passed to permit explicitly representation by nonlawyers.[34]

A United States district court in Massachusetts ruled that a state education agency has the right under the EAHCA to determine that an electronic recording of a hearing will be made instead of a written transcript. The court denied a parent's request for a written transcript, saying that there was nothing in the law or regulations obligating the state to make a written transcript.[35]

The Michigan Court of Appeals has confirmed the section of the regulations that permits a state reviewing officer to make his or her decision solely on the basis of the record of the local hearing; the decision to afford or deny the parties an opportunity to present additional evidence or oral or written arguments is totally within his or her discretion.[36]

Several federal courts have enforced the law's mandate that the decision of the state hearing or its review of a local hearing must be final. That is, the decision is binding on both parties unless an appeal for judicial review is made. The state may not subject the decision to additional review by state officials.

When Georgia's procedures made the decision of the state reviewing officer subject to approval or rejection by the state board of education, the United States Court of Appeals for the Fifth Circuit held the procedure violated the requirements of EAHCA. The court said:

> . . . Congress made unmistakably clear that the hearings provided by the Act were to be impartial and result in final decisions. If a State board may, at its discretion, reject the result of this process, the entire system of procedural safeguards is nullified at a single stroke.[37]

Other state and federal courts have taken the same view. Plaintiffs challenged a Nebraska statute they claimed allowed the state commissioner of education to review the decisions of state due process hearings.[38] Before litigation in this long-running case could be completed, however, the Nebraska legislature changed the law to conform with the EAHCA's requirements.[39]

The Supreme Court of Montana has said that the decision of the state-level hearing officer must be final, but it concluded that an apparent conflict in Montana did not in fact exist.[40]

The Student's Placement During Due Process

One of the most litigated sections in the EAHCA is the requirement that while the due process procedures are resolving a disagreement between a school district and the parent, the child must remain in the "then current educational placement" unless both parties agree to a change. This section of the law is frequently referred to as the "stay put" rule or the "status quo" rule.[41]

The courts are frequently asked to interpret the stay put rule because a parent who is unhappy with the school district's educational program unilaterally decides to withdraw the child from the public school program, to place him or her in a private school, and to sue to collect from the public schools the tuition costs for the private school. The United States Court of Appeals for the Fourth Circuit has established a rule for such cases, one that has been followed by many other federal courts.

In *Stemple* v. *Board*,[42] the parents of a handicapped child unilaterally removed her from the public school program, enrolled her in a private school, and then began administrative proceedings to recover from the school district the cost of the private school.

Under such circumstances, the court held that the stay put rule should apply to the parents. The court said the parent's duty to maintain the current placement of the child begins as soon as school officials make a decision about the identification, evaluation, and placement of a handicapped student and continues until the parent reaches a decision not to contest the decision, or if a contest is made, until it is finally resolved.[43]

The court explained the effect of the stay put provision in such cases:

> Taken literally, the language . . . creates a duty on the part of parents who avail themselves of the hearing and review provisions of [the law] to keep their child in his current educational assignment while the hearing and review provisions are pending, absent agreement between them and the educational authorities that some different arrangement be made. Of course, that duty may not be totally enforceable by the State, but it certainly negates any right on the part of parents, in violation of the duty and in the absence of agreement, to elect unilaterally to place their child in private school and recover the tuition cost thus incurred. [44]

The same basic rule—that parents may not collect for unilateral private school placements made in violation of the stay put rule—has been accepted by several other federal appellate courts.[45]

One, the Court of Appeals for the Seventh Circuit, has identified, however, two "exceptional circumstances" that may permit parents to ignore the stay put rule and still recover from the school district the cost of a unilateral placement for the child.[46]

The Seventh Circuit said these exceptional circumstances are: (1) where the current placement endangers the child's physical health,[47] and (2) when a school district acts in bad faith by failing to comply with the procedural protections in the law.

The court did not believe that Congress intended the stay put rule to prevent parents from protecting the child's interest in these two specific instances.

At least one lower federal court has supported the second exception by allowing a parent to recover the cost of an independent educational evaluation and private school placement when the school district repeatedly failed to give them the required prior written notice of their rights under the EAHCA.[48]

Due Process and the Disciplining of Handicapped Students

Perhaps the most surprising and controversial court decisions about the due process safeguards in the EAHCA address the question of whether or not the law requires a separate discipline system for handicapped students. The decisions are surprising because nothing in the congressional history of the EAHCA suggests Congress intended states to use different disciplinary procedures for handicapped children.

The cases have been controversial because many special educators believe that immunizing handicapped children from normal school disciplinary procedures does the children a great disservice by depriving them of the opportunity to learn that society will hold them responsible for their actions.[49]

Principals also point out that a separate disciplinary system for handicapped students imposes unreasonable requirements on school administrators.

This controversy over disciplinary procedures for handicapped children arises because the procedural safeguards in the EAHCA require that the parent be given written prior notice whenever the school proposes to change the handicapped child's placement and that they have available the full appeal process, including the right to an independent due process hearing and the right to judicial review, to challenge the decision.[50]

Therefore, if the school principal's disciplinary action against a handicapped student changes the student's educational placement, the parent can use the due process procedures in the EAHCA to appeal the action.

Most of the disciplinary sanctions used by principals do not affect the educational placement of the student; when, however, a student is suspended or expelled from school, it can be argued that the student's educational placement has been changed. Using that argument, some have asserted that state laws authorizing the suspension or expulsion of students for misconduct cannot be applied to handicapped students because the EAHCA contains the only procedure by which a handicapped student's placement can be altered.

If the parent of a handicapped student responds to a suspension or expulsion by seeking an independent due process hearing, the stay put rule of the EAHCA dictates the student must remain in school until the appeal process is completed. If such arguments are correct, the principal is effectively required to have two separate disciplinary systems as far as suspension and expulsion are concerned.

A United States district court in Connecticut was one of the first courts called upon to deal with this difficult issue. In *Stuart* v. *Nappi*,[51] the school board proposed to expel a learning disabled high school student with a history of behavioral problems for her participation in schoolwide disturbances. She filed a request with the school district for a due process hearing on her special education placement and asked the court for an injunction to prevent the expulsion.

Among her claims, she asserted her expulsion would violate the stay put rule of the EAHCA and that she was entitled to remain in her current educational program until all her due process rights were exhausted. She further argued she could not be expelled even after completion of all due process because to do so would deprive her of her right to a free appropriate public education in the least restrictive environment.

The judge recognized that the student's claims ran directly counter to the state law granting school officials power to expel students for cause. To confuse the case even more, the court had to consider a "comment" included in the EAHCA regulations that said the stay put rule "does not preclude the agency from using its normal procedures for dealing with children who are endangering themselves or others."[52]

The court eventually concluded that an expulsion would be a change in the student's placement and therefore could not take place during her due process challenge to the appropriateness of her educational program. The court also ruled that the school board could not expel the student in any case because that would deprive her of the right to a free appropriate public education under the EAHCA.

The court said the EAHCA prohibited the expulsion of disruptive handicapped students and substituted other procedures that must be followed to change their educational placement when necessary.

Having effectively immunized any handicapped student from expulsion, the court then went out of its way to express its regret at having intervened in the school's disciplinary process and to say how important it was for school officials to maintain ample disciplinary authority. The court explained the disciplinary power left to the principal.

> Handicapped children are neither immune from a school's disciplinary process nor are they entitled to participate in programs when their behavior impairs the education of other children in the program. First, school authorities can take swift disciplinary measures, such as suspension, against disruptive handicapped children. Secondly, [school officials] can request a change in the placement of handicapped children who have demonstrated that their present placement is inappropriate by disrupting the education of other children. The Handicapped Act thereby affords schools with both short-term and long-term methods of dealing with handicapped children who are behavioral problems.[53]

This decision established a rule that has been followed by other federal courts. That is, a handicapped student cannot be expelled under procedures established in state law for all public school students because expulsion is a change of placement. The EAHCA creates the exclusive means for changing a handicapped student's placement.

The handicapped student may, however, be suspended for a short term[54] because a short-term suspension is not a change in placement.

The United States Court of Appeals for the Fifth Circuit reached a similar conclusion about expulsion in the most widely-known case dealing with discipline of handicapped students. In *S-1* v. *Turlington*,[55] the court reviewed a case in which seven mentally retarded students were expelled from the Hendry County, Fla., public schools for disciplinary violations that under state law would have justified the expulsion of any student. The suit on their behalf claimed violations of rights protected by both the EAHCA and Section 504.

The Fifth Circuit generally agreed with the decisions in *Stuart* and other cases decided by federal trial courts[56] holding that expulsion is a change of placement that invokes the procedural protections of the EAHCA. The court, however, ruled that in certain circumstances a handicapped student can be expelled.

The court said that before a handicapped student can be expelled, a group of specially trained professionals, perhaps the IEP team or its equivalent, must determine whether or not the student's misbehavior was caused by his or her handicap. If the misbehavior was caused by the handicap, expulsion is not permitted, but the school officials may use the change of placement procedures in the EAHCA to move the student to a more restrictive educational setting.

If the misbehavior was not caused by the handicap, the student can be expelled but is entitled to use the full due process procedures in the EAHCA to contest the expulsion. The court also stated, somewhat enigmatically, that the school district may not completely terminate all educational services while the handicapped student is under expulsion.

Federal courts have accepted the rules governing expulsion that the Fifth Circuit created in *S-1*. The United States Court of Appeals for the Sixth Circuit, in *Kaelin* v. *Grubbs,*[57] in upholding a federal judge's decision that a 15-year-old mentally handicapped student had been improperly expelled from a Kentucky school district, based its decision on the premise that the boy was not afforded the due process procedures provided under EAHCA.

The Sixth Circuit reiterated the rule in *S-1* that a student may not be expelled if his or her misbehavior was a "manifestation" of a handicap, and said that when a handicapped student is expelled for behavior not related to his or her handicap, the school district may still not terminate all educational services.

Neither the Fifth Circuit in *S-1* nor the Sixth Circuit in this case explained what kind of services the school district must give the handicapped student who has been expelled.

The federal courts have expanded the coverage of the EAHCA's protections. One has held that an indefinite suspension is a change in placement,[58] and another has found that a learning disabled student who was distributing drugs in the school could not be expelled because his behavior was caused by his handicap.[59]

The federal courts have also reiterated the holding in *Stuart* that principals may suspend handicapped students for a short term without following the procedures in the EAHCA because a short-term suspension is not a change in placement. According to the United States Court of Appeals for the Sixth Circuit: ". . . It is well-settled that a handicapped child may be suspended temporarily without employing the provisions in 20 U.S.C. 1415. . . . These students may be suspended temporarily as long as they receive the procedural protections of *Goss* v. *Lopez,* 419 U.S. 565 (1975)."[60]

A United States district judge in Illinois strongly expressed the need for the principal to have the power to suspend unruly handicapped students. The case concerned a learning disabled high school student who was suspended for five days for using vulgar language in verbally abusing a teacher who had assigned him detention.

A local hearing officer supported the suspension, but the state superintendent reversed that decision. The superintendent's written decision blamed local school officials for the boy's misbehavior, saying that if he had to be suspended, it must be because the school staff had him in the wrong educational placement. In any case, according to the state superintendent, the courts would not permit the student to be suspended.

Judge Robert D. Morgan blasted the superintendent's opinion as "sophistry," saying the blame for such nonsense "rests not on 'the courts,' but solely on the State superintendent's own fallacious equating of a brief, temporary suspension with expulsion."[61] Judge Morgan went on:

> Any theory that some harm of the brief interruption of classroom work could outweigh the educational value of the suspension here can only be recognized as pure imagination, or a feeble attempt at rationalization of a preconceived notion that handicapped students, whatever the degree of handicap, are free of classroom discipline. That is not the law.[62]

A United States district court in New Hampshire upheld the suspension of a handicapped student for longer than 10 days when it found the misbehavior that caused the suspension was unrelated to the student's handicap and that the student had been provided the amount of due process required when any student is suspended for more than 10 days.[63]

The courts that have created separate rules for handling expulsions of handicapped students have gone to some pains to disavow any desire to place significant limits on the authority of school officials to discipline students.[64]

Notwithstanding these protestations, the judge-made law on expulsion virtually eliminates the possibility of expulsion as a disciplinary sanction for handicapped students. There is no evidence that Congress intended in the EAHCA to remove handicapped children from the ambit of state laws governing misbehavior by public school students. Nevertheless, the courts have created a protected class of students who are not subject to the disciplinary rules that govern other students.

At the same time, they have left many unanswered questions. For example, how can anyone determine in each case whether or not the student's misbehavior was caused by his or her handicap? What services must be provided to a handicapped student who is expelled for misconduct not related to his or her handicap? Hard questions that, as of now, may be left to the principal to answer.

The Right to Judicial Review

The EAHCA gives either party to a final due process hearing the right to appeal for judicial review. Obviously, the right has been used frequently.

Not only has this right opened the courts to the many substantive disputes we have already examined, but the right itself has been the subject of judicial interpretation about the specific procedures that must be followed and the authority of the courts when deciding cases.

The EAHCA says, in part:

> . . . any party aggrieved by the findings and decisions under subsection (c) of this section [final state administrative hearing], shall have the right to bring a civil action with respect to the complaint presented pursuant to this section, which action may be brought in any State court of competent jurisdiction or in a district court of the United States without regard to the amount in controversy. In any action brought under this paragraph the court shall receive the records of the administrative proceedings, shall hear additional evidence at the request of a party, and basing its decision on the preponderance of the evidence, shall grant such relief as the court determines is appropriate.[65]

Congress certainly did not want to encourage more law suits by authorizing judicial review of the final state administrative decision; rather, it hoped that most disputes over the educational program of a handicapped student would be settled through the administrative hearing process. To secure that goal, the law requires the parent to exhaust all administrative remedies before asking for judicial intervention.

Federal judges have generally been diligent in enforcing the rule that administrative remedies must be exhausted. The reasons the courts support the exhaustion doctrine, and the exceptions they have allowed, have already been discussed in some detail.[66]

To clarify even further the right to judicial review, two federal appellate courts have decided that although the law allows the parent to choose either a state court of competent jurisdiction or a United States district court, Congress did not intend that a parent be permitted to carry on litigation in both a state and a federal court at the same time.[67]

The United States Supreme Court, in its first decision about the meaning of the EAHCA,[68] gave federal and state judges some important guidance about how to handle disagreements about the educational needs of a handicapped student.

The Court said the job of the judge is to determine: "First, has the state complied with the procedures set forth in the Act? And second, is the individualized educational program developed through the Act's procedures reasonably calculated to enable the child to receive educational benefits?"[69]

The Supreme Court warned judges that the power of judicial review was not "an invitation to substitute their own notions of sound educational policy for those of the school authorities which they review," and that they should ". . . be careful to avoid imposing their views of preferable educational methods upon the states."[70]

Notwithstanding this advice, courts reviewing the final administrative decision under the EAHCA's due process procedures still exercise broad discretion and the power to make their own independent decisions.

Damages

The EAHCA allows the courts to grant "such relief as the court determines is appropriate"[71] when resolving differences between parents and school officials about the appropriate educational program for a handicapped student.

Does this language permit the court to award money damages to parents when a school district fails to provide an appropriate educational program, or otherwise violates the mandates of the EAHCA? The question has been the central legal issue in cases in which parents have tried to recover damages from school districts in the form of reimbursement for the expense of private educational services for the student; additional years of compensatory education for the student; and money for alleged equitable, compensatory, or punitive damages. The resulting court decisions have left an array of rules governing damage awards.

Most federal courts agree that Congress intended "such relief as the court determines is appropriate" to be primarily prospective injunctive relief, that is, court orders directing school districts to change past practices found to be a violation of the law or directing a specific educational program for an individual or group of handicapped students.

Several federal appellate courts have held that, without exceptional circumstances, Congress did not authorize the courts to award parents money damages when school district practices or programs are found not to have complied with the law.[72]

The courts have based their opinion that money damages are not available under the EAHCA on a review of the law's legislative history. They have found that Congress understood the severe financial limitations facing the states in the task of providing a public education for all handicapped students. Congress wanted to aid them with federal funding, not add to the burden by allowing courts to award damages for mistakes.

In addition, the lawmakers realized that precise diagnosis of the educational needs of handicapped students was a difficult undertaking, one in which some mistakes would inevitably occur. They chose to write extensive procedural safeguards in the EAHCA as the means of ensuring proper programs for handicapped students rather than allowing damages.[73]

The case of Bryan H. illustrates the reaction of some federal appellate courts to parental claims for money damages under the EAHCA.[74] The parents of 14-year-old Bryan sought money damages totaling $150,000 from school officials for allegedly failing to identify the boy as an emotionally disturbed child and failing to provide an appropriate program for him.

The United States Court of Appeals for the Fifth Circuit sustained the decision of a lower court to reject the parents' claim and award summary judgment in favor of the school officials. The court of appeals explained:

> . . . we join the Seventh, Eighth, and Eleventh Circuits, . . . in finding that the "appropriate relief" authorized by the EAHCA generally includes only prospective relief and that a damage remedy is not generally consistent with the goals of the statute. We hold, moreover, that when a school district in good faith attempts to provide a free appropriate public education to a handicapped child and has adequately complied with the procedures for determining the child's correct educational placement, it will not later stand liable to the parents for damages even if a court subsequently determines that the educational placement was incorrect.[75]

Using similar rationale, federal appellate courts have also rejected parental attempts to recover under the EAHCA money for equitable damages,[76] compensatory damages,[77] and punitive damages.[78]

Some parents have asked courts to award damages in the form of compensatory education—that is, additional years of free schooling beyond the student's normal eligibility.

The federal appellate courts do not agree about whether or not compensatory education can be awarded under the EAHCA. The Eighth Circuit, in 1982, held that compensatory education cannot be awarded because it is a form of damages for the school district's past conduct and is therefore barred by the Eleventh Amendment.[79]

The Seventh Circuit, after first agreeing with the Eighth Circuit that compensatory education is not available under the EAHCA,[80] has changed its mind and now believes that parents should be able to win an award of compensatory education because it is actually a prospective remedy very much like an injunction.[81]

The courts have also been unable to agree on cases in which parents ask for reimbursement for out-of-pocket expenses they have incurred in obtaining special education and related services for the student. In such cases, parents frequently assert that the services offered by the school district were not appropriate, or that the school district simply refused to provide services to the student.

The judge's decision may depend on the specific facts of each case, which can range from a complete refusal by a school district to comply with its legal obligations, to a unilateral decision by the parent to remove a student from a fully appropriate public school program in favor of a private school the parent prefers.

Because in these cases parents are seeking reimbursement for money they have actually spent for educational services rather than damages as a payment for past errors, the courts may consider the claim more a form of restitution than a demand for damages. The distinction may appear to be only semantics to the school district that has to pay.

Several federal appellate courts have decided cases in which parents moved a student from a public school program to a private school program without the school district's concurrence and then sought reimbursement for the cost of the private school. They have generally ruled that a school district has no obligation to pay for a private school for a handicapped student if it has provided or offered a free appropriate program in the public schools. Except in extraordinary circumstances, parents who unilaterally move a child to a private school while administrative due process or judicial review is underway forfeit any claim for reimbursement from public funds.

The Fourth Circuit's decision in *Stemple* v. *Board of Education*,[82] has been influential on this issue. The case concerned a multi-handicapped adolescent girl who had a long history of physical and emotional disabilities. She was a student for several years in a public school special education program that was satisfactory to her parents. They later became dissatisfied with her progress, unilaterally withdrew her from the public school, and enrolled her in a private day program at their own expense.

The parents then asked school officials to pay the cost of the private school and appealed through the administrative process when their request was denied. The case was finally decided by the Fourth Circuit Court of Appeals.

The Fourth Circuit emphasized that whenever parents are unhappy with the program the public schools are providing, they have access through the procedural safeguards in the EAHCA to challenge any decisions they dislike. The court said parents are, however, bound by the stay put rule to maintain the student in the current placement until their challenge is finally resolved. The court said:

> Thus we think that the statute means just what it says; and since there was a duty not to move the plaintiff until a final decision, plaintiff is lacking in any right to recover tuition payments for her parents' unilateral decisions to send her to a private school while she was seeking redress for the claimed violations of her rights.[83]

The court of appeals was not impressed by the parents' argument that they were exempt from the stay put rule because they enrolled the student in the private school before beginning the administrative appeal process. The court said the parent's duty to maintain the student in the current placement begins when the school authorities make a decision regarding the identification, evaluation, or placement of the student and continues until any due process ensuing from that decision is finally completed.

In a subsequent decision,[84] the Fourth Circuit reinforced the *Stemple* rule by holding that once a school system identifies a child as handicapped and proposes an IEP, the parents have a duty not to unilaterally alter the student's placement until any objections they have to the program proposed by the school are finally resolved through due process.

A number of other federal appellate courts have followed *Stemple* and denied parents reimbursement for unilateral private school placements.[85]

The United States Court of Appeals for the First Circuit, however, after first agreeing with the *Stemple* rule,[86] has adopted a different interpretation of the law. It believes parents should win reimbursement for a unilateral private placement if the court's final decision is that the private school they chose was appropriate for the student and the educational program proposed by the public school was not appropriate.

Borrowing from Emerson, the First Circuit implied the rule established in *Stemple* was based on a "foolish consistency," and the court ruled the stay put provision in the law is not mandatory but only directory. The court also suggested that when determining the amount the parents should recover for the cost of a unilateral placement, the lower courts should consider whether the parents made the transfer totally without consultation with school officials or only after efforts to negotiate a change with school officials failed.

The EAHCA, according to the court, envisions IEPs and placements cooperatively negotiated between parents and school officials, and a judge should therefore consider whether or not the parent made a good faith effort to win the agreement of school officials when determining the amount of the reimbursement they should receive.[87]

The United States Supreme Court, in *Burlington School Committee* v. *Department of Education*, 105 S. Ct. 1996 (1985), has rejected the *Stemple* decision and partially adopted the First Circuit's approach by holding that parents may recover the cost of a unilateral private school placement, even one made in violation of the stay put rule, if the court ultimately determines that the private placement they made was appropriate and that the program offered by school officials was inappropriate.

When the federal courts have denied parents the right to reimbursement for the cost of special education and related services obtained without the consent of school officials, they have emphasized that the no-recovery rule is based on the assumption that the school district has provided or offered an appropriate educational program for the student.

But how have the courts reacted to parent claims for reimbursement when the school district failed to provide appropriate services, denied services, or acted in bad faith by not according the parent the procedural safeguards required by the EAHCA? Under those circumstances, some federal courts have allowed the parents to recover their expenses.

For example, the Seventh Circuit Court of Appeals, in an opinion holding that damages are not generally available under the EAHCA, identified two "exceptional circumstances" that would justify a limited damage award, including only reimbursement for parents' out-of-pocket expenses for obtaining services.[88]

The Seventh Circuit said one "exceptional circumstance" is when the student's physical health would be endangered if he or she remained in the current placement during the appeal process. Congress expressed such a deep concern in the EAHCA for the welfare of the handicapped student that the court was convinced the lawmakers could not have intended the stay put rule to keep a child in a placement that would be a serious risk to his or her physical health.[89]

The second "exceptional circumstance" would occur if a school district acted in bad faith by an egregious failure to comply with the procedural protections in the EAHCA.[90]

The federal courts have also been willing to award reimbursement to parents when a school district simply refused to provide the services the law requires. The United States Court of Appeals for the First Circuit allowed the parents of a physically and mentally handicapped student to recover their cost for transporting him to and from school each day when school officials failed to provide transportation for him.[91]

The court did not limit the parents to their actual out-of-pocket expenses for the transportation, but also permitted them to recover the reasonable value of their own services for driving the student to and from school each day.

The trial court in this case had awarded the parents an additional amount for "equitable damages," which it said represented the dollars the school district saved during the period the student was unable to attend school because he lacked transportation.

The trial judge said the school should not be allowed to keep what he characterized as its "ill-gotten gains."[92] The court of appeals, however, reversed that part of the trial court's decision, saying such equitable damages are not allowed under EAHCA.

When a Nebraska school district sent a handicapped student home with a note saying that he could not return to school until he changed his behavior, the Nebraska Supreme Court found that the student had been denied the procedural safeguards of the EAHCA and approved an award reimbursing his parents for the cost of the private placement they made to preserve his health and safety.[93]

A United States District Court ordered parents reimbursed for a private placement of a hearing impaired child because the school district failed to give the parents the required written prior notice of their rights. Instead, according to the court, the school officials created a "procedural quagmire of Kafkaesque proportions" that denied the parents a fair opportunity to present their complaint.[94]

The United States Court of Appeals for the Ninth Circuit ruled that the failure of a school district to offer a student an appropriate educational program entitled the parents to recover the costs of a private school until an appropriate program was available in the public schools.[95] School personnel in this case failed to offer educational services in a public school with nonhandicapped children to a student suffering from cystic fibrosis and requiring periodic medication, lung suctioning, and reinsertion of a tracheostomy tube.

The school district recommended 1 1/2 hours of homebound speech therapy a week along with parent counseling. No academic instruction was included in the school's plan for the student. School personnel argued that the girl's handicap was so serious that she could not satisfactorily be taught in the regular classroom even with supplementary aids and services. The court disagreed; it said the student's successful attendance at a private school for a year proved she could be taught in a regular classroom. The school district's failure to offer a placement in the public schools violated the EAHCA.

The United States Supreme Court has not spoken on the right of plaintiffs to recover damages under the EAHCA, but it has taken note of lower court decisions allowing damages only in exceptional circumstances.[96] When the Court ruled that parents may not use Section 504 to obtain damages otherwise unavailable under the EAHCA, it commented on the reasons Congress had for not providing a damage remedy in the EAHCA.

According to the Court, Congress was aware of the financial burden the states faced in educating all handicapped students. One of the purposes of the EAHCA was to help relieve that burden; a damage remedy would have been inconsistent with that purpose.[97]

Can parents use Section 504 to win damages not available under the EAHCA? The lower federal courts have been confronted with many legal actions in which parents have alleged that the school district's actions have deprived the student of EAHCA rights and at the same time have violated Section 504. The Section 504 claims have often been added to the case for the sole purpose of allowing the parent to request damages or other forms of relief not permitted by the EAHCA.

In the past, some federal appellate courts have permitted parents to recover damages under Section 504 on the theory that the administrative remedies available to parents under Section 504 are not adequate to enforce the law and that Congress intended damages to be awarded by the courts in appropriate cases.[98]

The First Circuit has ruled that when the case concerns the obligations of the school district under the EAHCA, parents cannot use Section 504 to expand the very limited damage remedy of the EAHCA.[99] The Fifth Circuit has said that damages can only be recovered under Section 504 when the plaintiff can prove that the school officials intended to discriminate against the student.[100]

The United States Supreme Court has resolved these differences by holding in *Smith* v. *Robinson*,[101] that when the rights the parents seek to vindicate are covered under the EAHCA, they may not use Section 504 to evade Congress' decision not to provide for damages in the EAHCA.

Recognizing that allegations of Section 504 violations were frequently included in cases arising under the EAHCA for the purpose of justifying damages not available under the EAHCA alone, the Supreme Court said: "We are satisfied that Congress did not intend a handicapped child to be able to circumvent the requirements or supplement the remedies of the EAHCA by resort to the general anti-discrimination provision of §504."[102]

Attorney's Fees

May a court order a school district to pay the attorney's fees of the parent who is a successful plaintiff under the EAHCA? When Congress authorized the courts to award "such relief as the court determines is appropriate" did it intend to include awards of attorney's fees to a successful plaintiff? The answers can affect the school district's budget because the cost of the parent's attorney fees in some cases may far exceed the cost of the student's educational program. In one case, for example, the parents claimed more than $55,000 for five different attorneys.[103]

The EAHCA, however, does not explicitly authorize the awarding of attorney's fees to parents who convince a court that a school district has failed to provide the required free appropriate public education to a handicapped student. With this in mind, attorneys for parents have frequently added allegations of violations of Section 504 and Section 1983 of the Civil Rights Act of 1871[104] to cases brought under the EAHCA to justify a request for attorney's fees if the case is successful.

In July, 1984, the United States Supreme Court, in *Smith* v. *Robinson*,[105] sharply limited the ability of parents to recover attorney's fees in cases asserting the educational rights of the handicapped child. The Supreme Court held that Congress intended the EAHCA to be the exclusive means of enforcing the handicapped student's rights to a public education and it did not intend that parents be able to use either Section 1983 or Section 504 to win attorney's fees not allowable under the EAHCA. The court pointed out, however, that it was not ruling out the possibility of parents winning awards of attorney's fees, or requesting other remedies available under Section 504, when their suit was to protect rights to which the EAHCA does not apply.

The decision in *Smith* v. *Robinson* touched off a move in Congress to pass new legislation to reverse the effect of the Court's holdings.

A bill, taking the form of a proposed amendment to the Education of the Handicapped Act, was introduced to permit the awarding of attorney's fees, at the court's discretion, to successful plaintiffs under the EAHCA and to allow parents to use Section 1983 and Section 504 in EAHCA cases to expand the available remedies if the suit is successful.[106]

If this or similar legislation becomes law, it may encourage additional litigation against school districts and their administrators, add further to the complexity of special education law, and divert scarce tax dollars from educational programs to legal expenses.

Endnotes

1. Supra, Ch. 2.
2. 20 U.S.C. §1415 (b)(1)(A).
3. Ibid.
4. 20 U.S.C. §1415 (b)(1)(B).
5. 20 U.S.C. §1415 (b)(1)(C).
6. 20 U.S.C. §1415 (b)(1)(E) and (b)(2).
7. 20 U.S.C. §1415 (c) and (d).
8. 20 U.S.C. §1415 (e).
9. The Section 504 regulations, 34 C.F.R. §104.36, set out some of the same safeguards but permit compliance with the procedural safeguards in EAHCA to meet the requirements.
10. 20 U.S.C. §1417 (c); 34 C.F.R. §300.560 *et seq*.
11. 20 U.S.C. 1232(g).
12. In the Matter of W.L., No. D-9830 (Fam. Ct. New Castle Co., Del., June 27, 1982); 1982-83 EHLR DEC. 554:111.
13. Gebhart v. Ambach, Civ-82-224 (W.D. N.Y., September 12, 1982); 1982-83 EHLR DEC. 554:337.
14. Powell v. Defore, No. 81-71-MAC (M.D. Ga., January 11, 1982); 1981-82 EHLR DEC. 553:293. The school district later agreed to destroy the records in question. *See*, Powell v. Defore, 699 F.2d 1078, 1082 n.2 (11th Cir. 1983).
15. 34 C.F.R. §300.505.
16. OSE Letter to Jeffrey P. Grimes, March 20, 1980, 2 EHLR 211:187.
17. Hall v. Vance County, No. 82-1158-CIV-5 (E.D. N.C., November 23, 1983).
18. Infra, p. 54.
19. Hall v. Vance County, No. 82-1158-CIV-5 (E.D. N.C., November 23, 1983), 1983-84 EHLR DEC. 555:437, 443. *See*, Ruth Anne M. v. Alvin, 532 F. Supp. 460 (S.D. Tex. 1982)(recovery allowable for the cost of services the school district was obligated to provide but did not).
20. Supra, Ch. 1.
21. 20 U.S.C. §1415 (b)(2).
22. 20 U.S.C. §1415 (c)(d).
23. 300.506, 507, 508, 512.
24. S-1 v. Turlington, 635 F.2d 342 (5th Cir. 1981); *accord*, Foster v. District of Columbia, 523 F. Supp. 1142 (D. D.C. 1981).
25. Robert M. v. Benton, 634 F.2d 1139 (8th Cir. 1980). *See*, East Brunswick v. New Jersey, Civ. 81-3600 (D. N.J. July 7, 1982), 1982-83 EHLR DEC. 554:122.
26. Grymes v. Madden, 672 F.2d 321 (3rd Cir. 1982); *accord*, Vogel v. School Board, 491 F. Supp. 989 (W.D. Mo. 1980). *See*, Campochiaro v. Califano, No. H-78-64 (D. Conn. May 18, 1977) (local board member may not serve as hearing officer).
27. Vermont v. Kaagan, No. 82-243 (D. Vt. August 26, 1982), 1982-83 EHLR DEC. 554:349.
28. Helms v. McDaniel, 657 F.2d 800 (5th Cir. 1981).
29. DAS Bulletin #107, January 26, 1983, 2 EHLR 203:68.
30. Revised DAS Bulletin #107, January 16, 1984, 1 EHLR 104:221. See "EHLR Analysis: Impartiality of Hearing Officers (II)," 1982-83 EHLR DEC. pp. SA-69 to 72.
31. 34 C.F.R. §300.508
32. 34 C.F.R. §300.510
33. The dispute involved the state of Washington. *See*, "EHLR ANALYSIS: Representation by Laymen in Due Process Hearings," 1980-81 EHLR DEC. AC57.
34. Code of Virginia (1950), Section 22.1-214.

35. Roe v. Anrig, No. 80-1702-Z (D. Mass October 10, 1980).
36. Birmingham and Lamphere School Districts v. Superintendent, 328 N.W. 2d 59 (Mich. App. 1982).
37. Helms v. McDaniel, 657 F.2d 800, 805-6 (5th Cir. 1981).
38. Monahan v. Nebraska, 491 F. Supp. 1074 (D. Nebr. 1980).
39. Monahan v. Nebraska, 687 F.2d 1164 (8th Cir. 1982).
40. In the Matter of the "A" Family, 602 P.2d 157 (Mont. 1979).
41. 20 U.S.C. §1415 (e)(3).
42. 623 F.2d 893 (4th Cir. 1980), *cert. denied*, 450 U.S. 911 (1981).
43. *See also*, Rowe v. Henry, 718 F.2d 115 (4th Cir. 1983).
44. 623 F.2d 893, 897 (4th Cir. 1980).
45. Monahan v. Nebraska, 645 F.2d 592 (8th Cir. 1981); Stacy G. v. Pasadena, 695 F.2d 949 (5th Cir. 1983); Zvi D. v. Ambach, 694 F.2d 904 (2nd Cir. 1982); Mountain View v. Sharron, 709 F.2d 28 (9th Cir. 1983).
46. Anderson v. Thompson, 658 F.2d 1205 (7th Cir. 1981).
47. The court's example was a Texas case over the refusal of the school district to provide catheterization for a child. Tatro v. Texas, 516 F. Supp. 968 (N.D. Tex 1981).
48. Hall v. Vance County, No. 82-1158-CIV-5 (E.D. N.C. November 23, 1983), 1983-84 EHLR DEC. 555:437. *See also*, Jose P. v. Ambach, No. 79 C 270 (E.D. N.Y. January 5, 1982) (allowing parents to make unilateral placements at state expense to reduce a long waiting list for services in the public schools).
49. *See*, Brief of Appellants, Local Officials, S-1 v. Turlington, 635 F.2d 342 (5th Cir. 1980), 1979-80 EHLR DEC. 551:353, 362.
50. 20 U.S.C. §1415 (b)(1)(c), (d), and (e).
51. 443 F. Supp. 1235 (D. Conn. 1978).
52. 34 C.F.R. §300.513 comment.
53. 443 F. Supp. 1235, 1242, 1243.
54. The United States Supreme Court has said a suspension of 10 days or less is a short-term suspension. Goss v. Lopez, 419 U.S. 565 (1975).
55. 635 F.2d 342 (5th Cir. 1981), *cert. denied*, 454 U.S. 1030 (1982).
56. Sherry v. New York, 479 F. Supp 1328 (W.D. N.Y. 1979) (indefinite suspension); Doe v. Kroger, 480 F. Supp. 225 (N.D. Ind. 1979) (expulsion).
57. 682 F.2d 595 (6th Cir. 1982).
58. Sherry v. New York, 479 F. Supp. 1328 (W.D. N.Y. 1979).
59. School Board of the County of Prince William v. Malone, No. 83-862-A (E.D. Va. March 5, 1984), 1983-84 EHLR DEC. 555:504.
60. Kaelin v. Grubbs, 682 F.2d 595, 602 (6th Cir. 1982).
61. Board of Education of the City of Peoria v. Illinois, 531 F. Supp. 148, 150 (C.D. Ill. 1982).
62. 531 F. Supp. 148, 150 (1982).
63. Stanley v. School Administrative Unit No. 40, No. 80-9-D (D. N.H. January 15, 1980).
64. *See, e.g.*, S-1 v. Turlington, 635 F.2d 342 (5th Cir. 1981); Kaelin v. Grubbs, 682 F.2d 595 (6th Cir. 1982).
65. 20 U.S.C. §1415 (e)(2)
66. Supra, Ch. 2.
67. Coe v. Michigan, 693 F.2d 616 (6th Cir. 1982); Scruggs v. Campbell, 630 F.2d 237 (4th Cir. 1980).
68. Board of Education v. Rowley, 102 S.Ct. 3034.
69. 102 S.Ct. 3034, 3051.
70. Ibid.
71. 20 U.S.C. §1415 (e)(2).
72. Anderson v. Thompson, 658 F.2d 1205 (7th Cir. 1981); Miener v. Missouri, 673 F.2d 969 (8th Cir. 1982); Marvin H. v. Austin, 714 F.2d 1348 (5th Cir. 1983); Hurry v. Jones, 734 F.2d 879 (1st Cir. 1984).
73. Anderson v. Thompson, 658 F.2d 1205 (7th Cir. 1981); Marvin H. v. Austin, 714 F.2d 1348 (5th Cir. 1983).
74. Marvin H. v. Austin, 714 F.2d 1348 (5th Cir. 1983).
75. Marvin H. v. Austin, 714 F.2d 1348, 1356 (5th Cir. 1983).
76. Hurry v. Jones, 734 F.2d 879 (1st Cir. 1984).
77. Marvin H. v. Austin, 714 F.2d 1348 (5th Cir. 1983).
78. Marvin H. v. Austin, 714 F.2d 1348 (5th Cir. 1983).
79. Miener v. Missouri, 673 F.2d 969 (8th Cir. 1982), *cert. denied*, 103 S.Ct. 215 (1983).

80. Timms v. Metropolitan, 718 F.2d 212 (7th Cir. 1983)
81. Timms v. Metropolitan, 722 F.2d 1310 (7th Cir. 1983).
82. 623 F.2d 893 (4th Cir. 1980), *cert. denied*, 450 U.S. 911 (1981).
83. 623 F.2d 893, 898 (4th Cir. 1980).
84. Rowe v. Henry, 718 F.2d 115 (4th Cir. 1983).
85. Stacey G. v. Pasadena, 695 F.2d 949 (5th Cir. 1983); Zvi D. v. Ambach, 694 F.2d 904 (2nd Cir. 1982); Anderson v. Thompson, 658 F.2d 1205 (7th Cir, 1981); Miener v. Missouri, 673 F.2d 969 (8th Cir. 1982); Marvin H. v. Austin, 714 F.2d 1348 (5th Cir. 1983).
86. Doe v. Anrig, 692 F.2d 800 (1st Cir. 1982).
87. Doe v. Brookline, 722 F.2d 910 (1st Cir. 1983); Town of Burlington v. Department of Education, 736 F.2d 773 (1st Cir. 1984).
88. Anderson v. Thompson, 658 F.2d 1205 (7th Cir. 1981).
89. The court cited Tatro v. Texas, 516 F. Supp. 968 (N.D. Tex 1981), as an example.
90. *See*, Hall v. Vance County, No. 82-1158-CIV-5 (E.D. N.C., November 23, 1983), 1983-84 EHLR DEC. 555:437.
91. Hurry v. Jones, 734 F.2d 879 (1st Cir. 1984).
92. Hurry v. Jones, 560 F. Supp. 500, 508 (D. R.I. 1983).
93. Adams v. Deist, 334 N.W. 2d 775 (Nebr. 1983).
94. Hopkins v. Aldine, No. H 79-201 (S.D. Tex, April 3, 1984), 1983-84 EHLR DEC 555:412.
95. Department of Education v. Katherine D., 727 F.2d 809 (9th Cir. 1984).
96. Smith v. Robinson, 104 S.Ct. 3457, 3473 n. 24.
97. 104 S.Ct. 3457, 3474.
98. Miener v. Missouri, 673 F.2d 969 (8th Cir. 1982), *cert. denied*, 103 S.Ct. 125 (1982). *See also*, Powell v. Defore, 699 F.2d 1078 (11th Cir. 1983).
99. Hurry v. Jones, 734 F.2d 879 (1st Cir. 1984).
100. Marvin H. v. Austin, 714 F.2d 1348 (5th Cir. 1983).
101. 104 S.Ct. 3457 (1984).
102. 104 S.Ct. 3457, 3473. The Court added that plaintiffs are still free to sue under Section 504, including the possibility of winning damages, when it protects rights not covered by the EAHCA.
103. Monahan v. Nebraska, 575 F. Supp. 132 (D. Nebr. 1983).
104. 42 U.S.C. §1983.
105. 104 S.Ct. 3457 (1984).
106. The Handicapped Children's Protection Act of 1984, H.R. 6014 and S.2859, 98th Cong., 2d Sess.